THE
RAIDING
WINTER

THE
RAIDING
WINTER

M I C H A E L   R.   B R A D L E Y

PELICAN PUBLISHING COMPANY
GRETNA 2013

The word "Pelican" and the depiction of a pelican are
trademarks of Pelican Publishing Company, Inc., and are
registered in the U.S. Patent and Trademark Office.

Library of Congress Cataloging-in-Publication Data

Bradley, Michael R. (Michael Raymond), 1940-
  The raiding winter / by Michael R. Bradley.
    pages cm
  Includes bibliographical references and index.
  ISBN 978-1-4556-1817-0 (hardcover : alk. paper) — ISBN 978-1-4556-
1818-7 (e-book) 1. United States—History—Civil War, 1861-1865—
Cavalry operations. 2. United States—History—Civil War, 1861-1865—
Campaigns. 3. Tennessee—History—Civil War, 1861-1865—Campaigns.
4. Mississippi—History—Civil War, 1861-1865—Campaigns. 5. Forrest,
Nathan Bedford, 1821-1877. 6. Morgan, John Hunt, 1825-1864. 7. Van
Dorn, Earl, 1820-1863. 8. Wheeler, Joseph, 1836-1906. I. Title.
  E474.7.B63 2013
  973.7'33—dc23

                                                            2013008464

Printed in the United States of America
Published by Pelican Publishing Company, Inc.
1000 Burmaster Street, Gretna, Louisiana 70053

Contents

Introduction 7
Friday, December 12, 1862 19
Saturday, December 13, 1862 27
Sunday, December 14, 1862 31
Monday, December 15, 1862 37
Tuesday, December 16, 1862 41
Wednesday, December 17, 1862 45
Thursday, December 18, 1862 49
Friday, December 19, 1862 55
Saturday, December 20, 1862 59
Sunday, December 21, 1862 69
Monday, December 22, 1862 75
Tuesday, December 23, 1862 79
Wednesday, December 24, 1862 83
Thursday, December 25, 1862 87
Friday, December 26, 1862 93
Saturday, December 27, 1862 101
Sunday, December 28, 1862 107
Monday, December 29, 1862 113
Tuesday, December 30, 1862 119
Wednesday, December 31, 1862 125
Thursday, January 1, 1863 145
Friday, January 2, 1863 149
Saturday, January 3, 1863 151
Aftermath and Results 153
Appendix A: The Horsemen of the Confederate Raids 157
Notes 181
Bibliography 191
Index 197

Introduction

In December 1862, Confederate cavalry in the western theater mounted a series of raids that, collectively, were the most successful mounted operations of the entire war. Led by Gens. Nathan Bedford Forrest, John Hunt Morgan, Earl Van Dorn, and Joseph Wheeler, the Confederate horsemen demonstrated their ability to engage in a new type of highly mobile warfare. They also demonstrated the potential for this new style of war to disrupt both the tactical and strategic goals of their opponents. In just more than two weeks of active operations, the Confederate cavalry in the West shattered the strategic plans of both the Army of the Mississippi under Gen. Ulysses S. Grant and the Army of the Cumberland under Gen. William S. Rosecrans, forcing these two armies to remain stationary for five months. The cavalry also exercised tactical influence on Rosecrans's forces at the Battle of Stones River by destroying major elements of the supply train of the Army of the Cumberland and by forcing Rosecrans to detach large numbers of troops to guard his tenuous supply line. Neither the Union nor the Confederate cavalries ever matched this unprecedented burst of activity for the remainder of the war.

A New Style of Warfare

The Confederate forces in the West needed to find a formula for victory. They had suffered a major defeat at Forts Henry and Donelson in February 1862, a defeat that opened much of Tennessee and parts of northern Mississippi and Alabama to U.S. forces to harass and to occupy. The temptation to occupy a wider territory led the U.S. forces to make a mistake that almost proved fatal.

One of the basic principles of war is to concentrate your own forces in the face of the enemy. The U.S. high command ignored this principle and dispersed their forces. Gen. Don Carlos Buell moved from Nashville southeast toward Chattanooga with the main body of his forces, while Ormsby Mitchell took several brigades south toward Huntsville, Alabama. Grant took the main body of his command up the Tennessee River (that is, he headed south, since the river flows north) in the general direction of the vital railroad junction of Corinth, Mississippi, but then gave himself an inordinate amount of time to reinforce and reorganize his army.

While the U.S. forces were enjoying the fruits of their victories at Forts Henry and Donelson and were spreading out over the country to occupy it, the Confederates were scrambling to bring together forces from as far away as the Gulf and Atlantic shores to concentrate at Corinth, Mississippi. A gathering of forces at the railroad-junction town presented the possibility of defeating Grant at Shiloh and then turning on Buell. This plan almost worked. Grant and Buell recognized their danger with just enough time for Buell to move his men west, toward Grant. They arrived at the close of the first day of battle. If the men had arrived one day later, the history of the war might have been vastly different, and the Battle of Shiloh would have been pivotal in a very different way.

Almost is a very strong word. Buell did arrive in time to reinforce Grant and to contribute to a Union victory. The vital rail center at Corinth, Mississippi, soon was lost as well, and the Confederacy had to devise another plan to keep their hold on the western theater. For all of his battlefield failures, Maj. Gen. Braxton Bragg was a good planner. His reaction to the loss of Corinth was one such plan. Using the remaining railroad net, Bragg once again concentrated the C.S.A. forces, this time at Chattanooga, and launched a thrust into Kentucky.

The Kentucky Campaign offered another chance to reclaim what had been lost, and it did bring a higher morale and temporary relief from the pressure on Confederate forces. Most U.S. troops left Middle Tennessee, north Alabama, and much of Mississippi. But, so long as a U.S. garrison remained in Nashville, Bragg was denied the use of the Louisville & Nashville Railroad and so unable to supply his army during the winter months.

Had Sterling Price and Earl Van Dorn managed to capture Corinth, a line of supply could have been established along the Memphis & Ohio Railroad up to Kentucky, although this line would have been vulnerable to U.S. raids mounted out of Memphis. After the failure of the attempt to take Corinth, it was a foregone conclusion that Bragg would be forced to leave Kentucky before the army had time to move into winter quarters. A mobile Confederate army could feed itself off of the countryside in Kentucky, but a stationary army required a supply line.

Still, in November 1862, the Confederates were somewhat better off than they had been in the spring of that year. U.S. momentum had been checked. At the same time, Confederate counter-measures had proved to be ineffective. It was now clear that the Southern forces had insufficient numbers of infantry. Van Dorn had attempted to remedy this lack by dismounting cavalry during the Corinth Campaign, but the attempt had not proved to be effective.

It was also the case that the Confederate artillery was armed with too many lightweight, smoothbore guns to match the growing efficiency of the U.S. long arm. The one arm of the service in which the Confederates enjoyed superiority was the cavalry. In that branch, the South had both sufficient numbers and talented leadership. The Confederate forces available for strategic planning totaled about forty-five thousand infantry and approximately thirty thousand cavalry.

Following his narrow victory at Shiloh in April 1862, Grant had become mired in a controversy with his superior officer, Gen. Henry Halleck. The arguments and investigations associated with this squabble used up the summer, and an attack by the Confederates on Corinth in October—an attempt to coordinate with Bragg's Kentucky Campaign—won Grant's subordinate, William S. Rosecrans, a victory and an independent command. Grant, on the other hand, was stuck in St. Louis. When he was allowed to move, Grant was anxious to push south via Holly Springs and Oxford, Mississippi, on his way to attack Vicksburg. Grant needed a victory to restore his career.

With the Confederates weakened by their losses at Corinth and with their commander, Gen. Earl Van Dorn, discredited by defeat, the time seemed propitious. Grant moved east along the Memphis & Charleston Railroad, repairing the road as he went, and then turned south along the Mississippi Central Railroad. John Pemberton, the new Confederate commander, was badly outnumbered and had little choice except to fall back deeper into the territory that he was supposed to defend. It appeared as if Grant might achieve the military and personal goals he so desired.

William Starke Rosecrans knew what was expected of him, and he intended to deliver it. His predecessor, Don Carlos Buell, had been sacked because a lack of aggressiveness. Braxton Bragg had been allowed to lead his Confederate army over a large stretch of Kentucky for several weeks. For Rosecrans, it was Bragg's ineptness rather than Buell's skill that had led to a Confederate retreat from the bluegrass state. Bragg's problems in Kentucky were exacerbated by the continued U.S. occupation of Nashville, which deprived the Southerners of their best potential line of supply, the Louisville & Nashville Railroad.

Buell had not exploited Bragg's errors and had allowed the Southern army to return to Tennessee without serious harassment. The price Buell paid was to be removed from command, and Rosecrans understood the message. He would be aggressive and determined. Moving with his field army to Nashville, Rosecrans concentrated his forces, supplied his command, and made ready to march toward Murfreesboro, thirty miles to the south and east, where Bragg was waiting.

Big Names, Bigger Reputations

The Confederacy had to deal with aggressive and motivated opponents and most often had fewer men and resources with which to meet the challenge. To counter this weakness, the men in command developed strategies offset their losses.

The decision to use the cavalry to disrupt the enemy supply lines was not a new concept, but never before had the effort been done in so concentrated and effective a fashion. The Army of Northern Virginia's cavalry had made the first so-called raid of the war in June 1862, when James Ewell Brown Stuart led a picked brigade in a "ride around McClellan" as a prelude to the Seven Days' Battles. This event was more of a reconnaissance than a raid, since the men caused minimum disruption to Union supply lines and because the intentions of the movement were not to disrupt anything.

The eastern army's cavalry never developed the technique of the raid to the same extent as did the western cavalry. In part, this may be because the eastern theater was more compact and Union supply lines were less exposed. At any rate, the Confederate cavalry under Stuart, and later under Hampton, never devastated U.S. supply lines in the way that the western cavalry learned to do. Strikes behind Union lines by the Army of Northern Virginia cavalry caused brief disruptions of the flow of supplies, but at no time did a cavalry raid stop a U.S. advance in its tracks as the western cavalry did in December 1862. Neither Stuart, nor any of his subordinates, developed the skill and strategic ability to get behind Union lines, sustain themselves there for several days to a few weeks, wreak havoc, and then return unharmed. Such acts were the forte of the western cavalry.

A brief look at Stuart's cavalry in 1862 is instructive so as to demonstrate the differences in cavalry raids of the two theaters. On

August 22, 1862, Stuart was ordered to raid the communications of Gen. John Pope. Stuart recently had been embarrassed by being surprised in his bivouac by a U.S. cavalry force, which seized his hat and personal gear and nearly captured him as well. Stuart responded with a proposed raid with the military objective of destroying a railroad bridge over Cedar Run at Catlett's Station. Stuart and his men reached the station in secrecy and attacked with a night assault. They captured some prisoners and horses, and Stuart received the satisfaction of acquiring the dress uniform of General Pope. However, the railroad bridge went unscathed due to a heavy rain—no one could figure how to set fire to the structure. The raiders returned to Confederate lines on August 23 and had a good deal of fun with Pope's uniform.

Following the Maryland Campaign, which culminated in the Battle of Sharpsburg, Stuart made a raid to Chambersburg, Pennsylvania, for the purpose of destroying the bridge carrying the Cumberland Valley Railroad over the Conocheague River. This raid departed on October 10 and returned on October 12. During the course of those two days, Stuart's forces could not harm the bridge, since it proved to be constructed of iron, and did not damage either the Chesapeake & Ohio Canal or the Baltimore & Ohio Railroad, even though the raiders crossed each of these going in and coming out of U.S. territory.

On December 26, 1862, Stuart ordered his men to raid the Potomac River around Alexandria, Virginia, and many other villages and towns in the vicinity of Washington. The raiders returned to friendly territory on December 31, having accomplished nothing of importance.

The contrast between these colorless records of non-achievement in brief time periods and the record of the commands of Nathan Bedford Forrest and John Hunt Morgan is stark. With their determination and aggressiveness, either of these two men would have found a way to burn the Catlett's Station bridge, even in the midst of a thunderstorm. Morgan had had the ingenuity to destroy the twin tunnels on the Louisville & Nashville Railroad by running a line of cars into the tunnels and setting fire to the cars. At Chambersburg, a hot fire on the Conococheague Bridge would have warped and weakened enough of the structure to have put it out of service for some time.

Forrest and Morgan were more than ten years older than Stuart. Perhaps this age difference gave the western leaders more maturity and insight with which to meet the challenges they faced. Perhaps Forrest and Morgan were more focused on fighting than Stuart, or, as he styled himself, the Knight of the Golden Spurs. Whatever the reason, the western cavalry were masters of a new age of warfare in which cavalry became a mobile strike force with which to disrupt the composed net of the enemy. Stuart never learned this skill, and as a result he remained representative of a cavalry role which was obsolete, even in 1862.

The Confederate cavalry in the western theater created a new form of warfare due to their agility. Blitzkrieg, the concept of moving behind the enemy's front lines with a mobile, self-contained strike force that was developed by the Germans in World War II, has its origins in the raids carried out by Forrest, Morgan, Van Dorn, and Wheeler in December 1862.

The accomplishments of the Confederate cavalry of the western theater were made possible by a number of factors. One factor was the presence in the command structure of two charismatic commanders, Nathan Bedford Forrest and John Hunt Morgan. Forrest was still learning the craft of war, but even in those early years he was the stuff of legends. His foray to the banks of the Ohio River in 1861, his escape from Fort Donelson, the management of the evacuation of war material from Nashville, and his raid on Murfreesboro on July 13, 1862, had forged his reputation as a man who fought to win. Forrest also had established a reputation with Braxton Bragg as a man who did not function effectively when operating in conjunction with a regular army. This is curious, since Forrest had performed well in scouting and screening operations in 1861 and 1862, especially at Fort Donelson and at Shiloh. He had done an effective job with Bragg's army during the advance into Kentucky until, for some reason, Bragg lost confidence in Forrest and ordered him to turn over his command to John Wharton and to go back to Tennessee to raise more men. As part of this new command's duties, Forrest was to keep an eye the U.S. garrison in Nashville. Forrest carried out this task in compliance with his orders. Forrest could operate effectively in a traditional cavalry role and did so throughout the spring and summer of 1863, including the Chickamauga campaign.

The hold Forrest had on the men under his command is astounding. A nineteenth-century commentator, Lord Garnet Joseph Wolseley, said of them:

> They were reckless men, who looked on him as their master, their leader, and over whom he had obtained the most complete control. He possessed that rare tact—unlearnable from books—which enabled him not only effectively to control those fiery, turbulent spirits, but to attach them to him personally "with hooks of steel." In him they

recognized not only the daring, able, and successful leader, but also the commanding officer who would not hesitate to punish with severity when he deemed punishment necessary . . . They possessed as an inheritance all the best and most valuable fighting qualities of the irregulars, accustomed as they were from boyhood to horses and the use of arms, and brought up with all the devil-may-care lawless notions of the frontiersman. But the most volcanic spirit among them felt he must bow before the superior iron will of the determined man who led them. There was something about the dark gray eyes of Forrest which warned his subordinates he was not to be trifled with and would stand no nonsense from either friend or foe. He was essentially a man of action, with a dauntless, fiery soul, and a heart that knew no fear.

Forrest's counterpart, John Hunt Morgan, was at the zenith of his career during the winter of 1862-63. Successful raids into Kentucky and a series of victorious operations against U.S. garrisons at Gallatin and Hartsville, Tennessee, had made his name a name to be respected. The latter part of his career, beginning from his unauthorized raid across the Ohio River that resulted in his capture and the destruction of his command, would tarnish that patina of respect. Morgan also was inattentive to details, which resulted in his men being not well supplied, fed, or disciplined. This lack of discipline led to Morgan's death in 1864, when one of his pickets failed to stay awake and allowed a Union force to penetrate into the heart of Morgan's bivouac in Greenville, Tennessee, without being discovered. However, at the moment of December 1862, Morgan was a bright star in the Confederate firmament.

Morgan's background was quite different from Forrest's. Morgan had a first-class education, had enjoyed wealth he did not earn, and had always known financial stability. His personality was not as forceful as Forrest's, but he did attract the loyalty of his closest subordinates, and he was always a favorite among troops recruited from Kentucky.

It has been a trend for some historians to refer to Morgan and Forrest as guerrillas. This designation reflects either ignorance of the two men or of guerrillas or of both. Morgan and Forrest operated within the structure of the Confederate Army, spending much of their time in the routine duties of scouting and patrolling the front of the lines. It is argued that Morgan did not perform these duties well (and that charge contains truth), but being less than highly efficient as a cavalry commander does not make Morgan a guerrilla. Forrest was a strong believer in discipline. He, like Morgan, did not use guerrilla tactics but simply used innovative tactics of striking deep behind enemy lines and then returning to the main army. Both men had a talent for leading raids, and this talent earned them an admiring following. However, in no sense were they guerrillas.

In addition to charismatic officers such as Forrest and Morgan, the western Confederate cavalry benefited from the leadership of professional officers who were competent, if not spectacular. Gens. Earl Van Dorn and Joseph Wheeler both became exemplars of cavalrymen who attended to the routine duties of the mounted arm while still displaying a talent for strikes into the rear echelons of the enemy.

Earl Van Dorn was the son of a wealthy Mississippi plantation owner who was well connected with that state's aristocracy as well as with its political leaders, including Jefferson Davis. He graduated fifth from the bottom of his West Point class in 1842 (fifty-second out of fifty-six students) and saw service against the Native Americans and then in Mexico. During the Mexican War, he received a brevet promotion of captain. He returned to duty on the frontier and had risen to the rank of major when he resigned to join the Confederacy.

Van Dorn was a man of contradictions. In his public life, he placed great value on honor and duty, but in his private life, he thumbed his nose at the concept of marital fidelity and was noted for his extramarital affairs. Obsessed with a desire for glory, he failed in his first two major commands as a Confederate and was headed toward obscurity when he made his successful raid on Holly Springs in December 1862. He was a bold and dashing leader but not a loveable one, and he never created the bonds with his men that characterized the relations of Forrest and Morgan with their troops.

Van Dorn had not had a good battle until December 1862, when he led the raid on Holly Springs. He had been defeated at Elkhorn Tavern in Arkansas in the early part of the year and had failed in his attack on Corinth in the fall. By December, he had been left with an empty title and no real command. When regimental commanders in the Texas Brigade suggested that he be placed in charge of the Holly Springs expedition, Van Dorn was rescued from being left on the shelf. Following this successful move, Van Dorn and his command were ordered to Spring Hill, Tennessee, where he led the cavalry covering the left wing of the Confederates in Middle Tennessee. In this capacity, Van Dorn met several successes. Unfortunately, his career met an abrupt end when he advanced into very dangerous territory—the bedroom of another man's wife.

Joseph Wheeler thought of himself as a Southerner, but one must wonder why. His parents, of old New England stock, moved to Augusta, Georgia, when he was born, but lived there only briefly. Wheeler spent most of his early life in Connecticut. He was appointed to West Point and graduated from the Academy as nineteenth out of a class of twenty-two in 1859. He was assigned to the First Dragoons on April 22, 1861, following the beginning of the war at Fort Sumter and after Georgia had seceded. Following Shiloh, he transferred to the cavalry. During the Kentucky Campaign, he did a solidly professional job of scouting and screening the army. This performance won Bragg's approval, and Wheeler became his officer of choice for overall command of the cavalry of what was soon to be named the Army of Tennessee. However, as is so often the case, even a sterling performance of routine duties did not attract the public eye; Wheeler was not as well known or as popular an officer as Forrest or Morgan. Never, at any time during the entire war, did Wheeler prove himself as adept as Forrest and Morgan at striking deep behind U.S. lines and disrupting the service of supply. Wheeler made his best attempt as a raider in the late summer of 1864 in North Georgia, but went astray when he could not cross the Tennessee River to get at the rail lines in Middle Tennessee. Tactically, Wheeler did well in riding around Rosecrans's army more than once during the Stones River Campaign, and his destruction of supplies enhanced the chances of a Confederate success.

Because of his age, Wheeler was given the nickname War Child, which he earned by his personal involvement in battle. Over the course of the war, he was wounded three times, had sixteen horses killed under him, and saw thirty-six of his staff officers shot down at his side. This record of personal combat is second only to that of Forrest, yet Wheeler did not retain the reputation of a hard-riding fighter. Certainly, he never mastered the art of raiding behind enemy lines for extended periods of time and wreaking havoc in the same way Forrest and Morgan did. Following Chickamauga, Wheeler tried his hand at raiding during the Atlanta Campaign but without success. His greatest accomplishment against the U.S. cavalry came in his capture of Sherman's cavalry at Atlanta, when he stymied a raid against the rails supplying the town and, in the process, wrecked Sherman's horsemen.

The effective performance of routine cavalry duties, while valuable to the army, did not attract public attention. Perhaps his request to be buried at Arlington National Cemetery, following his service in the U.S. Army during the Spanish-American War, left a bad taste in the mouth of old Johnny Reb. At the time of Wheeler's death, many thought his dust should have rested among the gray-clad men he once led.

A Strategic Campaign

An important factor of the Confederate successes in December 1862 was the coordinated planning on the part of the high command. Pres. Jefferson Davis met with Gens. Joseph E. Johnston and Braxton Bragg and decided that blows against the U.S. supply lines were appropriate across the front that these two men covered. Bragg then initiated three of the successful cavalry moves. Although Bragg is often figured solely as a combat commander, one cannot reasonably overlook his successes as a strategic planner. His concept for the Kentucky Campaign was sound, and it achieved many of its strategic objectives in that the U.S. armies were forced to withdraw from much of the territory they had occupied during the first two-thirds of 1862. This withdrawal gave Confederates the opportunity to reoccupy valuable territory, which produced recruits, horses, and food. This temporary reoccupation of territory was the best possible outcome for the Confederacy. Without these victories, the Confederate presence in Kentucky could not have lasted through the winter. The presence of U.S. garrisons at Corinth, Mississippi, and Nashville, Tennessee, blocked the only available rail lines that could have supplied the Southern forces once they became stationary for the winter. In December, using the cavalry to deny U.S. forces the full benefits of their reoccupation of Tennessee built on Bragg's limited strategic success in the Kentucky Campaign and gave the Confederates forward momentum into 1863.

Not all of the planning for the successful use of the cavalry force originated at the top. The idea of destroying Grant's supply base at Holly Springs, Mississippi, originated at the regimental level and was passed up the chain of command. In this instance, the Southern forces were fortunate in the existence of capable and effective field officers who could both lead tactically and think strategically. The Confederacy was also fortunate that high-ranking officers were willing to listen to their subordinates and to act on their ideas.

In December 1862, all the right conditions existed to allow the Confederate cavalry to demonstrate the full extent of its battlefield abilities: concentrated forces, capable and motivated officers, and the ability to listen and take orders, which led to specific plans and coordinated attacks. The Confederates seized and exploited the opportunity to wreak as much damage as possible, much to the detriment of the plans of the U.S. army. This is the story of what was accomplished and of how it was done.

THE RAIDING WINTER

Friday, December 12, 1862

Murfreesboro, Tennessee

Jefferson Davis knew that his trip to Murfreesboro was necessary, but he wished it were not so. Tennessee and Mississippi, key components of the western theater, were both threatened again by Union forces. The first threat had been the result of the twin victories of Gen. Ulysses S. Grant in February 1862 at Forts Henry and Donelson. The fall of the forts had brought the U.S. Navy up the Cumberland River to the head of navigation with the army not far behind. This greatly hampered Confederate operations along the Tennessee-Kentucky border. Nashville became the first Confederate capital to fall and subsequently was so strongly fortified as to be beyond capture by assault.

Moving up the Tennessee River (heading south, since the river flows north), U.S. forces already had occupied parts of northern Mississippi and Alabama. A Confederate counter-move in April had held promise, but the Battle of Shiloh had not destroyed Grant's army. Indeed, the aftermath of the battle led to U.S. occupation of Corinth, Mississippi. At that town, the east-west line of the Memphis & Charleston Railroad crossed the north-south tracks of the Mobile & Ohio. The loss of this important rail junction was soon followed by the occupation of all of West Tennessee.

An innovative use of rail transportation allowed Braxton Bragg to shift his Confederate forces from Mississippi to Chattanooga, Tennessee, and then swing northwest across the Cumberland Mountains into Kentucky. This move relieved the immediate pressure on the western Confederacy, since most U.S. forces were drawn north to protect Louisville and other Ohio River towns. With Bragg back in Tennessee, the pressure on the western area had returned.

Because there was no railroad in Kentucky that Bragg could use to supply the Confederates once the winter arrived, the return of the army to Tennessee had been inevitable. Had Bragg led his men to victory at Perryville, the chances of a changed strategic situation would have been enhanced, as a Confederate win in the bluegrass might have so isolated Nashville as to cause a U.S. evacuation. But Bragg did not win at Perryville, and Confederate Secretary of War James Seddon was expressing a lack of confidence in the general. Unfortunately, so were a number of Bragg's subordinates.

So Davis had come to Tennessee to spread oil on the waters. He also came to confront the department commander, Gen. Joseph E. Johnston. Davis wanted infantry sent to Mississippi to enlarge the force under John C. Pemberton. Johnston opposed the idea. If infantry were detached from Bragg, Tennessee would be lost, Johnston argued. Cavalry raids on U.S. supply lines would be more effective in aiding Pemberton and would keep the Army of Tennessee on a numerical parity with the Army of the Cumberland.[1] Davis felt that a face-to-face meeting was needed to assert his authority and to settle the issue.

Gen. George Washington Custis Lee, the son of Robert E. Lee, accompanied Davis. Davis and Lee had been invited to stay at Oaklands, the home of Dr. and Mrs. Lewis Maney. The President was given a large room at the front of the new wing of the house. Hospitality was lavish, even though the war had begun to produce shortages in such items as coffee and sugar. Flour, rice, meat, and other commodities were still plentiful and available at reasonable prices. President Davis and General Lee were made comfortable and entertained in appropriate style.

Braxton Bragg took advantage of the happy occasion of the arrival of the president to issue General Orders No. 155. This order congratulated John Hunt Morgan on his feat at Hartsville on December 7, when Morgan's command had captured an entire U.S. brigade—more than 1,800 prisoners—at a cost to Morgan's command of 125 killed or wounded. Bragg noted, "The intelligence, zeal, and gallantry displayed by them will serve as an example and an incentive to still more honorable deeds. To the other brave officers and men composing the expedition the general tenders his cordial thanks and congratulations. He is proud of them, and hails the success achieved by their valor as but the precursor of still greater victories. Each corps engaged in the action will in future bear on its colors the name of the memorable field."[2]

The Old Natchez Trace, near Columbia, Tennessee

Nathan Bedford Forrest was not happy to be where he was, nor was he pleased with the destination to which he had been ordered. On December 10, he had received preemptory orders to march from Columbia, Tennessee, to make a raid on the Mobile & Ohio Railroad in West Tennessee. Forrest led a brigade composed of the Fourth Tennessee Cavalry under Col. James W. Starnes, the Eighth Tennessee commanded by Col. George G. Dibrell, the Ninth Tennessee under Col. J. B. Biffle, and the Fourth Alabama led by Col. A. A. Russell. Capt. Sam Freeman and his battery of six bronze cannon completed the force.

James Wellborn Starnes was a physician who had a taste for military life. He had served as Lt. Col. of the First Tennessee during the Mexican War. Forrest rapidly was coming to value the skills and leadership of Starnes, who, later in the war, often commanded a brigade. Jacob Barnett Biffle would be returning to his home on this raid. He was a farmer in Wayne County, not far from Clifton, and knew the roads in the area quite well. Alfred Alexander Russell was another physician who liked the military. From Stevenson, Alabama, he had fought in the Mexican-American War and brought to his regiment a reputation for being cool under fire. The coolness may have been both literal and metaphorical; Russell never unbuttoned his coat when going into battle. George Gibbs Dibrell was a merchant from Sparta, Tennessee, who had opposed secession but changed his mind when Lincoln called for troops.[3]

The regiments that Forrest had been ordered to lead into West Tennessee mostly were recent recruits, most of them having been in the service for only two months, although each regiment had a cadre of veteran troops. One of the men recalled that he had been under fire only once and that was in a minor skirmish. Forrest's main concern was their arms. For the most part, the men carried shotguns and flintlock muskets, most of which lacked flints. Many of the men had not received any weapons until November 2, when they had been issued a mixture of Enfield rifles, Belgian muskets, shotguns, and flintlocks leftover from the War of 1812 and dredged from the basement of various state arsenals.[4] There were approximately ten times Forrest's numbers' worth of soldiers in the U.S. garrisons in West Tennessee, so sending such poorly armed men into such an area seemed like a suicide mission.

The paucity of arms was exacerbated by the fact that the command would have to cross the Tennessee River on entering and exiting their target area. A poorly armed party would not be able to force a crossing—the river was normally a half-mile wide and, in the rainy winter season, might well be higher. It certainly would be swift. In addition, U.S. gunboats patrolled the river whenever the water level permitted.

Forrest had protested his orders from Bragg, pointing out that his men were not properly equipped for the mission, but the cavalry raids were part of Bragg's plan to aid Pemberton without dispatching any of his infantry. Forrest and his eighteen hundred men were on their way.

Their move was not unexpected by the Federal forces. As early as December 11, General Rosecrans had been sending out telegrams warning garrisons to "watch out for Forrest."[5] Gen. Jeremiah Sullivan, commanding U.S. troops at Jackson, Tennessee, had received the warning and had patrols watching possible river crossings in the direction of both Clifton, Tennessee, and Savannah, Georgia.

Jackson, Mississippi

Gen. John Pemberton felt some sense of relief for the first time in many days. He had been given the task of defending Vicksburg and knew that he did not have the manpower to do so. A U.S. Army under Ulysses S. Grant had established a base of supplies at Holly Springs, Mississippi, and had advanced all the way to Oxford, Mississippi. The best that Pemberton had done so far was to establish a strong line of earthworks on the banks of the Tallahatchie River in the hope that field fortifications would make his rather thin manpower more effective. By the time that Pemberton arrived, the manpower had weak and shaken morale. As if that were not enough, large numbers of Yankees were assembling at Memphis, presaging a move down the Mississippi to attack Vicksburg by water. The forces under his command could scarce resist a coordinated attack by two Federal forces at once.

Gen. Earl Van Dorn had commanded the army in Mississippi for several months and had accomplished nothing positive; indeed, he had almost wrecked the army in his campaign against Corinth in October. Not only had the battle been poorly fought but also the army had found itself almost trapped on its retreat. Only hard fighting and good luck had saved them. Following the Corinth campaign, the discouraged men had seen a huge army under Grant advance deep into the state with only token resistance. Van Dorn had about him the air of a failure. He had lost a battle at Elkhorn Tavern before coming east of the Mississippi and then had bungled the Corinth assignment. On top of that, people constantly questioned his personal behavior, especially his sexual exploits.

Pemberton was not happy with Van Dorn but had no one to take his cavalry commander's place when he became Van Dorn's superior officer. A curious request from the officers of the Texas Brigade had landed on Pemberton's desk, and he had decided to act on it. Now, he had the satisfaction of knowing that he was taking his best chance of stopping the U.S. juggernaut.

Holly Springs, Mississippi

Ulysses S. Grant was not a happy man. He had penetrated deep into Mississippi but was having trouble managing his command. His staff included many men who were not experienced in managing military affairs, and President Lincoln did not approve of his choice of subordinates. While Grant moved overland towards Vicksburg, he had ordered William Sherman to lead a column down the Mississippi from Memphis and to converge on Vicksburg by water. At this critical point, Lincoln had ordered Grant to replace Sherman with John Alexander McClernand. Grant deliberately chose the slowest possible means of communication to inform McClernand of the change—rather than send a telegram, Grant dispatched a letter, which did not reach its intended destination. Either Bedford Forrest intercepted it somewhere in West Tennessee, or it simply was never delivered.[6]

Grenada, Mississippi

Riding through the winter weather, thirty-five hundred Confederate cavalrymen made their way toward Grenada, Mississippi. These men were in surprisingly good spirits for men who had known nothing but military reverses and who reported to a general whose name was synonymous with defeat. Earl Van Dorn, the loser at Elkhorn Tavern and at Corinth, had been chosen to lead a cavalry force to the rear of Grant's advancing army in order to capture Holly Springs, Mississippi, the supply base on which Grant depended for his continued advance toward Vicksburg. Riding toward Grenada was the Texas Cavalry Brigade of fifteen hundred men commanded by Col. John S. Griffith, the Tennessee Cavalry of twelve hundred led by Col. William H. Jackson, and a brigade of Missouri and Mississippi riders numbering eight hundred under Col. Robert M. McCulloch.[7]

The plan to assemble the cavalry force and to place Van Dorn in charge had not come from the Confederate high command. It had originated at the regimental level. On December 5, the regimental commanders of the Texas Brigade wrote to General Pemberton. They said,

> The undersigned officers of the First Texas Brigade of Cavalry, disclaiming any desire to dictate to the Commanding General any plan or line of operations he should pursue, would yet beg leave modestly to suggest the propriety of a cavalry expedition into the enemy's rear. We are the more bold to do so, and have less fears of the misconstruction of our motives, when we remember that you have been so recently placed in command over us; and that the multitudinous cares incidental to your responsible position have necessarily, thus far, precluded an examination of the position of the enemy, and, as to what is the best employment in which the cavalry, under your command, can be engaged. We, therefore, respectfully submit, if you will fit up a cavalry expedition, comprising three or four thousand men, and give us Major General Earl Van Dorn, than whom no braver man lives, to command us, we will penetrate the rear of the enemy, capture Holly Springs, Memphis, and other points, and perhaps, force him to retreat from Coffeeville; if not, we can certainly force more of the enemy to remain in their rear, to protect their supplies, than the cavalry could whip if we remain at the front.

The letter was signed by Col. John S. Griffith, who commanded the brigade, E. R. Hawkins, who commanded the First Texas Legion, J. H. Broocks, major in the First Texas, Jiles S. Boggess, lieutenant colonel of the Ninth Texas, and Jack Wharton, captain of the Sixth Texas.

Griffith was from South Carolina but had lived in Mississippi and Arkansas prior to the war. He had commanded troops at Wilson's Creek and would stay in combat until the end of the war. John Mason "Jack" Wharton was a Marylander who had been in Kansas prior to the war. He joined the Sixth Texas and later came to command that regiment, but Wharton often had trouble disciplining his men. John H. Broocks, a veteran of the Mexican War and a successful businessman, had gone into farming just prior to the war. Jiles Boggess had been a Texas Ranger and knew a good deal about fighting even before he became a Confederate cavalryman. Edwin Robert Hawkins was a native of North Carolina and a physician who had lived in Texas since 1858. His unit was sometimes referred to as the Twenty-Seventh Texas.[8]

Pemberton had not only received the letter, he had acted on

it with remarkable speed. In sum, three brigades of Confederate cavalry went riding off though the rain toward Grenada.

Franklin, Tennessee

A U.S. force consisting of the Third Kentucky, Seventh Pennsylvania, and Fourth Michigan struck Confederate pickets about two miles from town. The pickets were part of a four-hundred-man force commanded by Col. Baxter Smith of the Eighth Tennessee. There was a sharp skirmish along the banks of a tributary of the Harpeth River, but the Yankee line was too long for Smith to contain. Outflanked, he fell back toward Triune. Hearing of the withdrawal, Gen. John A. Wharton, commanding a division under Wheeler, sent reinforcements and asked Gen. Patrick Cleburne to send infantry to help check the move. After destroying a gristmill, the U.S. forces withdrew. General Wharton asked to be allowed to keep his forces south of Franklin so as to keep them more concentrated.[9]

Oxford, Mississippi

The war was turning ugly. Hostility toward the South was becoming more pronounced among U.S. troops, and Grant struggled to keep his men disciplined. Unauthorized killing of civilians and looting of houses was common, not only to forage for food but also to steal items of value. One young woman recalled her mother returning to her home following the passage of Grant's army only to find that all their possessions had been ruined. "Bonfires had been made of books, most of the family china had been trampled underfoot, carriage and horses taken, provisions confiscated."[10]

In response to this deteriorating situation, Grant issued Special Field Orders No. 21. "Distress and almost famine having been brought on many of the inhabitants of Mississippi by the march of the two armies through the land, and humanity dictating that in a land of plenty no one should suffer the pangs of hunger," it was ordered that pro-Union families should sell goods to families based on need, while pro-Confederate families should pay a special tax to help support this effort. Grant appointed officers to see that the funds collected were used properly.[11]

Having taken this step, Grant bade goodbye to his wife, Julia, their son, Jesse, and his wife's female slave, Julia, and moved to join his advanced forces at Oxford.

Saturday, December 13, 1862

Murfreesboro, Tennessee

It is to be hoped that Davis got a good night's sleep, because Saturday was a very busy day. His first order of business was to meet with Braxton Bragg. This would not be a smooth meeting, because Davis's purpose was to see to it that the division commanded by Maj. Gen. Carter L. Stevenson was dispatched immediately to Mississippi. Bragg did not want to give up those eight thousand men. Confederate intelligence reports estimated that General Rosecrans had just more than forty-three thousand men at Nashville. There were ten thousand to fifteen thousand more U.S. soldiers in various garrisons guarding the supply line of the Army of the Cumberland. If Bragg could keep his army intact, he would have had about forty-five thousand men to oppose Rosecrans when the two met on the battlefield. The department commander, Gen. Joseph E. Johnston, had already made his opinion clear—the dispatch of Stevenson's division would jeopardize the Confederate hold on Tennessee.

Davis viewed the strategic picture differently. Not only did he have emotional ties to Mississippi, a state to which he had moved as a child, but he also saw the fertile farm lands of the region as a bread basket that could both feed the western Confederacy and produce a surplus for the eastern region. Davis also was under pressure from Mississippi political leaders, who complained that so many men had been moved from their state to protect other areas.

The outcome of the meeting with Bragg was never in serious doubt. Davis was the commander in chief, and he took that role seriously. He was quite willing to heavily supervise the Army of Tennessee if it was needed to achieve his goals.

Following the meeting with Bragg, he has a more pleasant duty. Davis promoted John Hunt Morgan and Roger W. Hanson of the Second Kentucky Infantry, known as the Orphan Brigade, to brigadier. He also promoted Patrick R. Cleburne to major general and gave him command of the unit formerly commanded by Simon Bolivar Buckner, who had transferred to East Tennessee.

Following that business came a grand review of the three divisions making up Gen. Leonidas Polk's corps. Polk described the event to his wife a few days later, saying, "the review was a grand affair; everything went off admirable, and he [Davis] was highly gratified with the result—said they were the best appearing troops he had seen, well appointed and well clad. The sight was very imposing, and, as it was my corps, was very gratifying to me."[1] The *Murfreesboro (TN) Daily Rebel Banner* said that the troops were much impressed with Davis, who presented himself with a "manly form" and an "unpretending style."[2] One rather imagines that most of the soldiers gave a sigh of relief when the whole thing was over and they returned to their camps for a little relaxation.

Once the presidential party returned from the review, Davis and the ranking generals at Oaklands ate dinner. As a finishing touch to the evening, a crowd of townspeople serenaded Davis, who responded with a few remarks.

On the Banks of the Tennessee River, Clifton, Tennessee

Forrest and his eighteen hundred men were wet through and through, and the village of Clifton offered no shelter. The men had been on the road from Columbia, Tennessee, since December 10 and had ridden the last several miles through a pelting icy rain. President Davis must not have actually seen Forrest's men when he called the Army of Tennessee "well-appointed," because most of the men were lacking rubber blankets. Most problematic, however, was the fact that they lacked proper weapons.

The only properly armed unit in the entire command was Freeman's Battery, which included as a supernumerary a young lieutenant whom Forrest was not sure he liked. John W. Morton had shown up at Forrest's headquarters a few days before, asking to join Freeman's Battery. Forrest thought Morton to be a spy from Bragg's headquarters and called Morton "a whey-faced boy."[3] As the command reached Clifton, the twenty-year-old Morton approached Forrest: "General, I have recruited enough men to crew two guns but I have no cannon. Will you issue us some shotguns? When we cross the river we intend to fight and Colonel Starnes says we can fight under him." Forrest looked into Morton's eyes, liked what he saw, and said, "You be patient. I'll get you some cannon."[4]

One piece of good news was that Maj. Nicholas Nichols Cox was on hand with a few dozen men of his recently organized partisan ranger battalion. Like Forrest, Cox had been born in Bedford County, Tennessee, but had grown up in Texas. Cox returned to Tennessee to attend the law school at Cumberland College and practiced law in the West Tennessee area when the war began. Cox was a veteran officer who had lost his position when his first regiment was reorganized. Upon returning to his home territory, he raised another unit.[5]

When Forrest got his orders to march into West Tennessee, he had sent word to Cox to take his men to Clifton and to start building flat boats to ferry the men across the river. Cox and his men had been working on the banks of a flooded slough called Carroll Creek, out of sight of any U.S. gunboats that might have passed along the river. They had constructed two small craft out of hewn logs, each one capable of carrying twenty-five men and their horses. Forrest would depend on these two crude craft, hardly more than rafts, to get across a river nearly a half-mile wide with a strong current.

Dan Beard recalled,

> When we arrived at Clifton we turned to the right and bivouacked in the bushes, without fires for fear of attracting the gunboats, which we had learned were patrolling the Tennessee River. The river had a good boating tide and appeared to be rising. During the night we moved down closer to the river bank, which was a bluff. A little beyond the middle of the river was an island, or large sandbar, on which were several men and horses and two or three big, bright fires. On our side they were pushing the horses off the bluff, about ten feet clear fall into the swift, icy cold water, the horses going out of sight. When they came up the poor brutes would swim round in a circle until one would see the fire on the sandbar and strike out for it. Some would never see the fire at all, but exhausted themselves trying to climb the same bluff they were pushed off of. We lost eight horses.[6]

The command soon abandoned this attempt waited for daylight, at which point they began crossing in the flatboats.

Grenada, Mississippi

Van Dorn's Confederate cavalry continued to move into Grenada. The lines further to the west, where the U.S. was making their advance, were quiet, and the cavalry was able to leave that front unnoticed. Their arrival in Grenada put them well to the east of the main U.S. forces, leaving the way north open. Only cavalry was assembling. Unlike Forrest, Van Dorn had decided that artillery would have slowed his movements too much, even if the guns and caissons were double-teamed. This decision would negatively affect the outcome of at least two engagements in the coming days.

In part, this decision reflects Van Dorn's inexperience as a cavalry raider. Forrest and Morgan both had learned that even light artillery was very effective in the bombardment of fortified buildings, timber stockades, and blockhouses. In part, the decision reflects the fact that Van Dorn knew that he was going to be confronting a larger number of U.S. soldiers at a much closer distance than either Forrest's or Morgan's raids. While all the raiders would be deep behind U.S. lines, Forrest and Morgan would be in an area more removed from the major fighting forces. Van Dorn would have Grant to his south and Sherman, in Memphis, to his west. It was a more dangerous situation whose success depended on constant, rapid movement.

Sunday, December 14, 1862

Chattanooga, Tennessee

Jefferson Davis caught the train from Murfreesboro to Chattanooga. He had other stops to make before returning to Richmond and had to be on his way. The President told the War Department that he believed that the activities of the Confederate cavalry under Gen. Joseph Wheeler kept the Army of the Cumberland cooped up in Nashville and that the projected raids would soon damage U.S. communications.

Actually, two of the raids were already underway, but Davis either did not know or chose not to mention this fact. He did relay to Richmond that public opinion in East Tennessee and northern Alabama was not enthusiastic about Confederate prospects.[1]

Clifton, Tennessee

Forrest was anxious to get across the river. The longer he stayed at Clifton, the better the chance that he would be discovered by a passing gunboat. If that were to happen, all of the garrisons on the west side of the river would be expecting him. In much of West Tennessee, the Tennessee River had cut its course deep into the soil, making the river bordered by dirt bluffs ten to twenty feet high. At Clifton, a ravine led down to the river, providing the town with a landing for boats carrying goods and for a ferry that led across to a flat place on the opposite bank. This was the site where Forrest began to cross his men. Forrest sent lookouts a mile and more both up the river (south) and down the river (north) to give warning if the smoke of an approaching boat appeared. Freeman positioned his guns to protect the crossing, and then the men led the horses down the road to the ferry landing and herded them onto the flatboats.

After each flatboat was loaded, the men pulled it up the river for several hundred yards, remaining close to the shore to take advantage of the slack water. When they reached an appropriate distance, they rowed toward the middle of the stream, where the current was stronger. By using the rudder carefully, the force of the current carried the boat to the opposite shore. Once everyone was unloaded, the soldiers repeated the process in reverse. With only twenty-five men and horses to each boat and with only two boats, the crossing was a slow process.

As the men assembled on the west side of the river, they moved inland and took up positions in a defensive perimeter to guard against any surprise. Using a skiff, Forrest crossed and re-crossed the river repeatedly, keeping an eye on the entire procedure.

Franklin Pike, outside Nashville, Tennessee

Lt. S. H. Stevens was a Federal officer in the Chicago Board of Trade Battery and knew that the horses of his command needed forage. He secured a pass from General McCook, countersigned by General Negley, to go outside the lines and see what he could take from the farmers of the region. He took with him three wagons and six men. Hearing that fodder was to be had at a particular farm, he led his detail there. While loading the wagons, a patrol of Confederate cavalry attacked the foraging party, taking all of the enlisted men prisoner except for Stevens, who fought his way out of the barnyard and escaped on foot.[2]

Lt. Stevens's report demonstrates one of the difficulties confronting both sides during this period of the war. Stevens used the word "guerrillas" to describe the party that attacked him. Many of the Confederate cavalry had been recruited in the fall of 1862 and had not been issued complete uniforms. Even when uniforms had been issued, men often supplemented their clothing with garments sent from home. As a result, the Confederate cavalry did not have a very military appearance, and it was easy to dismiss them as armed civilians. Obviously, many of the men who followed Forrest out of West Tennessee were recruits who later would fight at Parker's Crossroads in the civilian clothes they wore when they left home. As the war progressed, the issue of who was and was not a guerrilla became increasingly contentious.

Grenada, Mississippi

All of the troops chosen for the Holly Springs raid were in town. Every farrier in each of the brigades was busy shoeing horses, officers inspected arms, and commanders issued three days of cooked rations along with sixty rounds of ammunition per man. These were all sure signs of an imminent movement, but, as yet, no one knew the destination.

Murfreesboro, Tennessee

John Hunt Morgan had been a widower for seventeen months, but that was about to change. On the evening of this day, he would marry Martha Ready, the daughter of former Congressman and Mrs. Charles Ready Jr. Morgan's first wife, Emily, had died in July 1861 following a lengthy illness. In February 1862, as Nashville was being evacuated and Morgan commanded troops near Murfreesboro, Mr. Ready had invited Morgan to dinner. Seeing that he was "rather sad," Martha—called Mattie by her friends—had sung for him. From that time on, a romance had blossomed.

When Confederate forces returned to Middle Tennessee later in 1862, Morgan and Mattie began to exchange notes and visits. Morgan's fame was growing, as he had made an extensive and successful raid into Kentucky and then captured the U.S. garrison at Gallatin, Tennessee.

At age thirty-seven, Morgan stood six feet in height and weighed 185 pounds, making him considerably larger than most men of the time. Mattie was twenty-two and was considered a striking beauty with high spirits. She was described as being a very attractive young woman of medium height, a shapely figure, fair and creamy complexion, large blue eyes, and dark hair. She had attended Soule College in Murfreesboro and the Nashville Female Institute. One of her early suitors had been Samuel Scott Marshall, whom she met in Washington. Although refused as a husband, Marshall returned to visit the Ready family when his Illinois regiment occupied the town in 1863.

Charles Ready was a very successful attorney who had been mayor of the town twice and had served Tennessee as a U.S. representative. He was a member of the Whig Party. The Ready family was an old Rutherford County family, well established in land holdings and with a number of slaves to work their land. The Ready house, a brick, two-story building surrounded by an ornamental garden, stood just a few feet off of the courthouse square in Murfreesboro.

Mattie had a single attendant in her wedding party: her sister, Alice. In the group were Gens. Braxton Bragg, William

Hardee, Benjamin Franklin Cheatham, Roger Hanson, and John Breckinridge, former U.S. vice president. Gen. Leonidas Polk, the Episcopal bishop of Louisiana, donned his vestments over his uniform and conducted the service.

Basil Duke recalled, nearly fifty years later,

> All the officers of high rank who could reach Murfreesboro had assembled for the wedding, General Bragg among them. Distinguished civilians were present in great numbers. The house was packed with people to its full capacity and decorated with holly and winter berries, the lights from lamps and candles flashed on the uniforms and the trappings of the officers and were reflected in the bright eyes of the pretty Tennessee girls who had gathered. The raven-haired, black-mustached Morgan in his general's uniform looking like a hero of chivalry, the bride, a girl of rare beauty, tall, dark-haired and blue eyed with a creamy complexion and perfect features and standing before them, to perform the ceremony, in his full military uniform, Bishop Polk, himself a general of the Confederate Army and Bishop of the Episcopal Church. Miss Ready's bridal dress was one of her best ante-bellum frocks, for it was not possible at that time to purchase material for a trousseau. I am certain the bride could not have worn anything more appealing but she did wear a bridal veil. General Morgan's attendants were as dashing a set of young soldiers as any bride could wish at her wedding.

Following the wedding ceremony, the guests ate an elaborate dinner featuring turkeys, hams, chickens, ducks, game, and all the vegetables a Southern winter garden could provide. Colonel Ready's cellar still held enough good wine to provide numerous toasts for the couple, and three regimental bands provided a serenade.

Not far from the site of the wedding festivities was the camp of the Second Arkansas Infantry, where Andrew J. Campbell was resting. Campbell was to make Mattie a widow 630 days later. Deserting the Confederate army, Campbell joined the Thirteenth Tennessee Cavalry of the U.S. army. On September 4, 1864, in an attack on Morgan's position at Greenville, Tennessee, Campbell shot Morgan dead.[3]

Water Valley, Mississippi

Col. T. Lyle Dickey, commanding a division of U.S. cavalry, received orders from General Grant to take about eight hundred picked men and move east to raid the Mobile & Ohio Railroad.

Colonel Dickey took his Second Brigade, saw that the men were issued fifty rounds of ammunition and enough hardtack and salt for six days, and led the men off on his mission. Grant dispatched other cavalry forces in other directions in order to attract the attention of the Confederates. In all, Grant committed about half of his total cavalry force to this raid and the diversions associated with it. Dickey kept his men in the saddle all night in an attempt to get beyond the Confederate lines.[4]

Monday, December 15, 1862

Clifton, Tennessee

As soon as it was light enough to see, Forrest's men began to ferry more men and horses across the river. By Monday morning, the majority of the men were across, and Forrest was concerned about providing more security for his bridgehead. A couple of miles from the ferry landing on the western shore, the road leading north descended a long hill. At the top of this hill, the road, which had been running east-west, turned ninety degrees to the north. Forrest sent a heavy detail of men to this position with orders to drag logs from the surrounding woods and to pile them into a crude breastwork. Then Forrest sent for John Morton. Since the young artilleryman had expressed an eagerness to fight, Forrest ordered him to borrow two guns from Captain Freeman's battery, return the cannons to the opposite shore of the river, and place them at the advance position. Morton eagerly obeyed.

Some time in the early afternoon, the flatboats made their last trip to the west side of the river. As Forrest led his men away from the river, a few men rowed the boats back to the Clifton bank and up Carroll Creek and sunk the boats. About three hundred men who were sick or whose horses were weak stayed behind to guard Clifton.

The column of cavalry rode about eight miles, to the vicinity of Bath Springs, and stopped for the night. Well away from the river and possible discovery by passing gunboats, officers announced that fires were permitted. This was a great luxury for the cold, wet men, who had bivouacked without fires since arriving at Clifton on December 13.

Grenada, Mississippi

A dapper man on a fine black mare rode along the column of Confederate cavalry assembled at Grenada. The roar of cheers swept over the town. The soldiers had recognized Earl Van Dorn.

The general had not been successful at Elkhorn Tavern, he had failed to take Corinth, he was not in good standing with the high command, and there were numerous questions as to how well he liked the intimate company of women. Still, the cavalry liked him and were glad to be under his command.

Although they had no artillery in their ranks, the men were prepared to give someone a hot time—each soldier had been issued a bottle of turpentine and a box of matches. Overall, the command traveled light: the men carried three days' cooked rations, ten days' salt rations, and sixty rounds of ammunition. One pack animal followed each company, and no wagons were in the column.[1]

The cheering men did not ride very far on this day but just across the Yalobusha River. There, they waited while Generals Van Dorn and Pemberton consulted to determine if any last-minute changes were required in their plan. The men bivouacked in the cold rain to await daylight.

On the Murfreesboro Pike, near Nashville, Tennessee

Lieutenant Colonel Hawkins of the Confederate Army had the mission of going into U.S. lines under a flag of truce for the purpose of arranging the passage of a group of civilians through the lines to Nashville. He reached an outpost of the Fourth Michigan Cavalry, where companies H and M were on duty. Stretching east from the main outpost were a number of men posted as chain pickets, whose purpose was to provide a long, thin chain to keep watch so that no one slipped past the main picket post. Hawkins waited for an officer of equal rank to escort him to the general in command of the sector.

Because Hawkins had arrived under a flag of truce, the men of the two Michigan companies assumed a general truce was in effect. Those in the main outpost put down their carbines and gathered in clusters, gossiping and drinking coffee. Many of the chain pickets dismounted and made themselves comfortable.

Suddenly, the Rebel Yell split the air, and the First Alabama Cavalry swept over the post. All the men on chair-picket duty were hustled off as prisoners. Letters demanding an explanation from each other flew back and forth between Rosecrans and Bragg until the Battle of Stones River began a few weeks later.[2]

Murfreesboro, Tennessee

At eight o'clock, the band struck up a waltz in the courthouse just across the street from the Ready house, the site of John Hunt

Morgan's wedding to Mattie Ready the day prior. The Sixth Kentucky and the First Louisiana regiments were sponsoring a ball in honor of the couple. Candles illuminated the hallways of the courthouse, and regimental colors hung from the walls. Behind each candle, a polished bayonet had been set as a sconce to reflect the light, and a chandelier of bayonets holding candles hung from the ceiling of the main hall. Cedar trees and vases of flowers decorated the dance hall. The festivities went on until dawn.[3]

Pontotoc, Mississippi

Colonel Dickey's Yankee raiders rode into Pontotoc at about 9:30 a.m. The weather had turned nasty, and a cold rain was falling steadily. Dickey only had encountered some small Confederate scouting parties, so he divided his force. A group of one hundred men under Major Coon was sent to Coonewar Station to destroy a railroad bridge in the vicinity. The rest of the command rode on toward Tupelo. The roads were so poor and the stream crossings so difficult that they spent the rest of the day reaching their destination.

The detachment under Major Coon had some excitement. Passing on through Coonewar, they approached Okolona. They captured a few prisoners, cut the telegraph wires, and hid themselves to ambush a train due at the station a few minutes later. Somehow, the engineer on the train knew of the ambush and put the engine in reverse. Coon and his men gave chase, firing at the train only to find that the passengers were firing back! One of Coon's men jumped onto the engine but was forced to jump right back off. Following the escape of the train, Coon decided to rejoin the main force, which he reached at about daylight the next day.[4]

Tuesday, December 16, 1862

Near Bath Springs, Tennessee

Nathan Bedford Forrest was moving rather slowly. He had worked hard to get his command across the Tennessee River and had moved inland far enough to avoid observation by gunboats, but he didn't seem to be in a great hurry to move against the garrisons of U.S. troops in the area. No doubt this struck some of his followers as odd—delay only gave time for the opposition to reinforce their positions and to gather troops for a pursuit; however, curiosity was not sufficient motivation to cause anyone to risk the general's famous temper by asking him what he was doing. At any rate, the men moved only eighteen miles farther, through Scotts Hill and Shady Hill, following the Old Stage Road.

The reason for the slow movement was quite simple: defective ammunition. The incessant rain of the past several days had damaged much of the ammunition that the men carried, especially the percussion caps. Forrest was ever resourceful. He contacted a friend behind U.S. lines and had arranged for this person to bring a supply of fresh caps. In some way, Forrest always seemed to know someone on whom he could call for a guide, for accurate information, or for needed material. On the night of December 16, a citizen arrived at Forrest's headquarters with fifty thousand caps for shotguns and pistols. Now, Forrest could fight.[1]

Cavalry Headquarters, Murfreesboro, Tennessee

Gen. Joseph Wheeler had a division of cavalry with which to cover the front of Bragg's army. These men were kept as close to the U.S. lines as possible, patrolling the area from the Franklin Pike to the west all the way to the Lebanon Pike to the east. This post kept an eye on all the roads leading from Rosecrans's position at Nashville to Bragg's position at Murfreesboro. The division consisted of Wheeler's own brigade and that of Brig. Gen. John A. Wharton. Buford's brigade and a small brigade under Pegram guarded the Confederate supply line. Wheeler and Wharton were harassing daily the foraging and scouting parties sent out from Nashville.

Morgan's command had been permitted a rest period after their attack on Hartsville on December 7. Now, they began to move north and northeast of Murfreesboro to the village of Alexandria, embarking on what would later be known as the Christmas Raid. From there, a good road led to the Cumberland River.

Grenada, Mississippi

Van Dorn led his men east and northeast all day and through most of the night. The roads were muddy and the streams were high, but the men were glad to be moving against the enemy. There was a good deal of speculation as to their destination, and most of the gossip in the ranks centered on catching a band of raiders that Grant had sent against the Mobile & Ohio Railroad.[2]

As the column sloshed along the muddy roads of Mississippi, Van Dorn was about to get a good idea of what waited for him in Holly Springs. When the raid had been confirmed, Van Dorn had tasked Captain Baxter, commander of a company of scouts, to penetrate the town of Holly Springs and bring back information on the numbers and disposition of U.S. troops there. One of the medical doctors in the town acted as a spy, gathering information useful to the Confederates and passing it on as opportunity offered.

Captain Baxter selected one of his scouts named Spencer to make the trip. Spencer asked D. J. Hyneman, seventeen years old, to accompany him on this duty, because the two had worked together on prior assignments. The two men reached a farmhouse about three miles outside of Holly Springs but found that the man of the house had taken the family livestock south to protect it from Yankee foragers. A one-armed veteran of Manassas was living with the family, and he offered to help the two scouts slip through the sentry lines into town. As soon as it was dark, the three set off, successfully entered Holly Springs, and reached the house of the doctor. It was agreed that the doctor would gather the needed information the next day and would then get a pass to go out into the country to "see a sick man." The three soldiers then slipped back out of town and returned to the farmhouse. Spencer and Hyneman spent the next day hiding in the woods, just in case a patrol came to the farmhouse. They returned after sunset, met the doctor, got the information they needed, and began their ride to meet Van Dorn.[3]

Wednesday, December 17, 1862

In the Vicinity of Shady Hill, Tennessee

With percussion caps ready to be issued to his men, Forrest was now ready to fight. It all fell to a question of timing. If his command moved out early, it could easily reach Lexington that day; however, there would be no chance of surprise, as any attack would have begun in the coverless afternoon. The best plan, Forrest decided, would be to remain in place, resting the men and horses until midday. Then, a cautious afternoon's march would allow the command to bivouac just outside of Lexington and attack at dawn.

Forrest reached a position about two miles from Beech Creek on the outskirts of Lexington just as dark was falling. He sent a scouting party forward, and it determined that a U.S. outpost was located at the crossing of Beech Creek. Forrest knew what to do, and he knew the man to do it. A courier called Capt. Frank Gurley to the general's side.

Gurley had entered the war as a member of the Kelley Rangers, a company raised in Huntsville, Alabama, by a Methodist minister, David C. Kelley. This company became part of Forrest's original regiment, and Gurley made a name for himself as a good soldier. In the summer of 1862, Forrest's original regiment was broken up, and the Alabama companies became the nucleus of Col. A. A. Russell's Fourth Alabama. Russell commissioned Gurley to go behind U.S. lines into his home territory and to recruit a company. As he was engaged in this endeavor, a target of opportunity came his way. Gen. Robert L. McCook's brigade was passing through Madison County, Alabama, on its way toward Winchester, Tennessee. Gurley and eight men shadowed the move. McCook had diarrhea and was riding in a light wagon but had not turned over command to a subordinate. Near New Market, Alabama, McCook ordered the wagon driver to go on ahead of the column so he could locate a place to bivouac. When the wagon had gotten about eight hundred yards ahead of the marching men, Gurley and his eight men attacked. In the ensuing fight, McCook was mortally wounded.[1]

Now Gurley was captain of a company of the Fourth Alabama, had led the advance on Lexington, and had provided the scouts that had located the U.S. position at Beech Creek Bridge. A man who would challenge a brigade with just eight men was precisely the man Forrest wanted to open the fight at Lexington. Upon reporting to Forrest, Gurley was directed to be back at headquarters an hour before daylight with thirty men chosen from his company.

In truth, the presence of Forrest near Lexington was not a secret. Col. Robert G. Ingersoll, commander of U.S. forces in the area, knew that Confederates were in the vicinity. That morning, a Captain O'Hara of the Second West Tennessee Cavalry (U.S.) had led a patrol of seventy men from Lexington to the vicinity of the Tennessee River. He did not make contact with Forrest, but he did bring back a report that 3,000 infantry, 800 cavalry, and six guns had crossed the river near Clifton. Colonel Ingersoll telegraphed Grant that his pickets and those of the Confederates were in sight of each other. Ingersoll had 200 men from the Eleventh Illinois Cavalry, 272 men of the Second West Tennessee, two guns of the Fourteenth Indiana Light Artillery, and 200 recruits from the Fifth Ohio Cavalry.[2]

Near Houston, Mississippi

The men under Van Dorn had only a brief halt during the night of December 16. Their commander was anxious to get as far east as possible to minimize the chance that his move would be discovered. They made a brief halt near noon at the village of Houston to allow the men to eat and to feed their horses.

Following this brief respite, the gossip among the men flared up anew. Instead of continuing east toward the Mobile & Ohio Railroad where the Yankee raiders were, the column turned north toward Pontotoc.[3] This change in direction kept tongues wagging until another fifteen miles had been covered and the column stopped for the night.

Holly Springs, Mississippi

Ulysses Grant was disgusted. More specifically, he was disgusted with speculators who had followed his army south in hopes of buying cotton and sending it north. Since the war had begun, the supply of cotton had disappeared, and New England textile-mill owners were desperate for the fiber. The profits to be made by sending cotton north were enormous. But the South was no longer the land of cotton. Beginning in 1862, the Confederate government had urged the growing of foodstuffs, and the Southern farmers had followed this suggestion. Thousands of bales of cotton became mere dozens. This meant that the speculators were feverish in their activities. In Grant's mind, the cotton speculators all had one thing in common—they were all Jewish. He had already forbidden any speculators to follow his army across the Mississippi state line, but the town of Holly Springs was, somehow, full of them. So, Grant issued General Orders No. 11:

> The Jews, as a class violating every regulation of trade established by the Treasury Department and also department orders, are hereby expelled from the department within twenty-four hours from the receipt of this order.
>
> Post commanders will see that all of this class of people be furnished passes and required to leave, and any one returning after such notification will be arrested and held in confinement until an opportunity occurs of sending them out as prisoners, unless furnished with permit from headquarters.
>
> No passes will be given these people to visit headquarters for the purpose of making personal application for trade permits.[4]

C.S.A. Cavalry Headquarters, La Vergne, Tennessee

All across the front guarded by Wheeler's cavalry, patrols clashed and attacked U.S. foraging parties. Officially, these were unimportant skirmishes. For some of the participants, however, it was their last day on Earth.

Nashville, Tennessee

A U.S. court of inquiry decided that Gen. T. T. Crittenden had not been at fault in surrendering the men at Murfreesboro to General Forrest on July 13, 1862 (five months earlier). It was found that Crittenden had been surprised, not through any fault of his own, but because subordinates did not follow his orders to increase the size of the pickets outside town.

Crittenden lost all of his command to a numerically inferior force, even though he had been in command for only one day when the surprise attack was made.[5]

Forrest had been quite pleased with the July 13 raid—it had occurred on his forty-first birthday. It had also caused Gen. Don

Carlos Buell to stop his advance toward Chattanooga and look to his supply lines instead.

Harrisburg, Mississippi

Colonel Dickey and his tired men camped near Harrisburg, which he described as "a deserted town."[6] During December 16 and 17, his men had wrecked thirty-four miles of track on the Mobile & Ohio, including one large bridge. He had captured military supplies and had loaded eight wagons with his spoils. The only inhabited farm in the vicinity was owned by a certain Mrs. Sample.

She used slaves as overseers, provided a school for slave children (even though she had twice been called into court for doing so), and made sure that all of her workers could read and write. This not only made them more efficient but also satisfied Mrs. Sample's religious requirements, because they could read the Bible. Indeed, she conducted religious services for them every Sunday. The two slave overseers had control of all the business affairs, including harvesting and selling her crops and purchasing the necessary supplies for the next year. Mrs. Sample pointed out to the raiders that if they took more food than they needed, they were taking it out of the mouths of her slaves. She and Colonel Dickey agreed that only what was needed would be taken, and the soldiers exercised great care in not despoiling the corn cribs and smokehouses. As a good Confederate, Mrs. Sample knew that she could not receive compensation for what she lost, but she made quite an impression on the U.S. officers who met her—so much so that Colonel Dickey sent her an ox-cart loaded with salt from Oxford, Mississippi. When Dickey's column rode on the next day, not one of the Sample slaves left with them.[7]

Thursday, December 18, 1862

Near Lexington, Tennessee

As ordered, Gurley arrived at Forrest's headquarters while it was still dark. According to an eyewitness, Forrest told Gurley, "Take the thirty men I ordered and advance down the Beech Creek road. You will find their pickets at a bend in the road. Drive them in. If necessary, order up the rest of your company or more of Russell's regiment until you get enough to drive them and keep driving them. Don't let them stop."[1] Obviously, Forrest had already adopted the strategy of "get 'em scared and keep 'em scared."

Gurley was soon on his way. It was light enough to see but still before sunrise when Gurley struck the U.S. pickets. It became a running battle back to Beech Creek, and there Gurley met a check. The floor had been taken up from the bridge, and a number of men from the Second West Tennessee Cavalry (U.S.) commanded by Col. Isaac Hawkins were posted on rising ground on the far bank. Gurley called up more of the Fourth Alabama, and Hawkins's men left in a hurry except for a few sharpshooters, who tried to delay the repair of the bridge. The gray soldiers took rails from a nearby fence, made a temporary flooring of them, led their horses across, and cleared the enemy from the banks of the stream.[2]

As soon as he had a few men across the stream, Gurley took up the pursuit. The U.S. troops had fallen back to a fork in the road just outside Lexington, and there they made a stand. The Eleventh Illinois took position alongside part of the Fifth Ohio and elements of the Second West Tennessee. Two guns of the Fourteenth Indiana Light Artillery, commanded by Lt. John W. H. McGuire, reinforced the line.

This was a strong position, and, as at the Beech Creek bridge, the defenders checked the Confederate assault. As more men arrived to support an attack, Gurley left Colonel Russell to lead a frontal assault, while Gurley led his company off to the left into a wooded ravine. Using this cover, Gurley burst onto the left flank of the U.S. line while Russell charged from the front. The Union line collapsed, and the skirmish then became a horse race to see how many prisoners the Confederates could take. However, the victory was not without cost to the Confederates. Gurley later recalled, "The gunners stood by their guns and died like soldiers. The last shot was fired just as we reached the battery, and my first sergeant, J. L. P. Kelly, and his horse were blown to atoms by the explosion. With the taking of the guns, the cavalry gave away in a stampede and many of them were captured."

Robert Ingersoll, the commander of the U.S. forces, had brought 773 men into the fight by his own reckoning. Out of his men, 11 were killed, eleven wounded, and 147 men captured along with 70 horses and the two guns of the Fourteenth Indiana.[3]

Ingersoll was a nationally known lecturer who spoke widely about his agnosticism. He also had a quick wit. When ordered to surrender, he asked, "Is this you Southern Confederacy for which I have so diligently searched? Then I am your guest until the wheels of the great cartel are put in motion. Here are my Illinoisians; the Tennesseeans have fled."[4] Indeed, one of the results of Forrest's raid was to dampen the Unionist feelings that were growing in the counties along the Tennessee River. The economies of these towns were linked by water transportation to St. Louis, and their politics before the war had included a wide streak of Whig sentiment.

The "great cartel" kept Ingersoll a "guest" of Forrest for almost two weeks. During that time, Ingersoll was free on his personal parole and took his meals with Forrest's staff. Dr. J. B. Cowan, the son of a Cumberland Presbyterian minister, made a believer of Ingersoll. The captive colonel did not become a convert to Christianity, but he did gain a conviction of Cowan's infallible ability to fill an inside straight! When Ingersoll was released, Cowan loaned the now-broke agnostic one hundred dollars to get home—one hundred Confederate dollars. Cowan kept the greenbacks he had won.[5]

Capt. Charles Anderson, adjutant to Forrest, captured the chaplain of the 122nd Illinois, the Rev. M. J. J. Carmichael. The Reverend was something of an abolitionist but took his capture with good grace—until Anderson told him that the fine saddle on the preacher's horse was now spoils of war. Carmichael protested that it was a gift from his congregation, so Anderson decided to use religion, not force, as his argument. "Preacher, don't your flock want you to follow the example of our Lord?" "Yes," Carmichael replied. "Well," said Anderson, "the Scriptures only tell of one time

Jesus rode a horse, and on that occasion it is clearly stated that he mounted the animal bareback. If that is the way Jesus did it, I am sure your congregation would want you to do the same."

A. J. Lacy of the Eighth Tennessee summed up the engagement quite well in a letter to his parents: "Wee went to Lexington in Henderson County, there we run the Yankees and captured two pieces of artillery and a good many prisoners."[6]

The two cannon became famous as the "Bull Pups" of Morton's Battery. Morton described their acquisition: "But in the eyes of Lt. Morton, serving with a portion of a borrowed battery, the proudest achievement of the whole affair was the capture of the two guns, rifled Rodmans, which were given into his possession, enabling him to return to Captain Freeman the two which had been loaned. No subsequent capture ever brought the same pleasure as did that of these two well-equipped guns, and they accompanied him and gave good service during the remainder of the war."[7]

Pontotoc, Mississippi

At about noon, the Confederates reached Pontotoc, and there occurred one of the moments that they would clearly recall as grizzled old men. News of their approach preceded them, and when the wet, hungry men reached town, they found the townspeople lining the streets cheering and holding out food. One of the troopers recalled:

> Passing through the beautiful town of Pontotoc the hungry troopers were enthusiastically welcomed by the noble and patriotic citizens of the place, and trays, dishes, and baskets of the choicest edibles were offered on all sides and pitchers of wine and milk as well. No halt was allowed and the men pursued their mysterious way munching the welcomed "grub" dispensed by the fair hands of Pontotoc's good and beautiful and noble heroines. O, Peerless ladies of Pontotoc, through the mists of twenty years becloud the mind's eye and interminable leagues intervene between us, the courtly Griffith, and his surviving Rebels salute you.[8]

As the last men of the Confederate rearguard left Pontotoc licking crumbs from their lips, the advance guard of the raiders who had attacked the Mobile & Ohio Railroad rode into the opposite end of town. Colonel Dickey had first learned of the Confederate presence in Pontotoc at about noon, when people leaving the town told him that Rebel cavalry was in town. Dickey destroyed the wagons he was using to transport captured goods, turned his men to the north on a by-road, and then moved by country roads northwest toward Pontotoc, hoping to pass north of the town and thus to escape notice. While making this move, some slight skirmishing took place with flank guards of Van Dorn's column, and Dickey deduced that his opponent was actually moving north instead of trying to intercept his force. By this stage of his operation, Dickey's men rode jaded horses, and avoiding conflict was very desirable. As the blue soldiers moved into Pontotoc, they could still see the Confederate rearguard in the distance. Dickey was pleased to see the Confederate column depart at right angles to his line of march and immediately ordered couriers to ride to Grant at Oxford with news of what he had seen.

The presence of the Yankees was reported to Van Dorn, who was equally pleased to find Dickey behind and not ahead of him. A fight only would eat up valuable time and alert more U.S. forces to his presence. When news of Dickey's force was reported to Van Dorn at the head of the column, he is reported to have said to the courier, "You go back and tell the officer in command of the rearguard that behind me is exactly where I want the Yankees." Dickey sent a patrol to follow Van Dorn to make sure that the Confederates did not turn back on him, and, when they continued northward, Dickey called in his men and continued west. On reaching a suitable bivouac, the colonel was dismayed to learn that the couriers he had ordered for some reason had never left for Grant's headquarters. He sent two more men out into the deepening darkness.[9]

Van Dorn led his men on to New Albany, crossed the Tallahatchie River, and made camp for the night. The slumbering men were awakened at about midnight by a torrential rain that flooded their campground.[10]

Night, near Jackson, Tennessee

Forrest understood the value of time, so he did not dawdle at Lexington. A detachment remained to parole the enlisted prisoners and to scour the field for weapons. The rest of the command pressed on toward Jackson, driving in all of the U.S. pickets on the various roads leading into town. The sound of locomotive whistles made it obvious to all of Forrest's men that trains were coming into Jackson from north and south, no doubt with reinforcements gathered from the small garrisons along the rail routes.

At Jackson, the Mississippi Central Railroad branched off from the Mobile & Ohio. The Mississippi Central led south via Bolivar and other towns to Holly Springs, where General Grant had his supply base. The Mobile & Ohio led north from Jackson to Humboldt, where it crossed the Memphis & Ohio, which ran northeast to southwest. Forrest needed to sever these routes in order to prevent more men from reaching Jackson and to isolate the smaller, vulnerable garrisons. At 8:00 p.m., Forrest began his move. Col. George Dibrell went with one hundred men to Humboldt with orders to capture the first station above Jackson, wreck any trains he could find, and destroy the tracks. Dibrell found his target at Webb's Station, where 101 U.S. soldiers were posted in a stockade. Under the threat of artillery bombardment, these men were soon prisoners. Dibrell's men exchanged their flintlock muskets for the modern weapons of the captured garrison. Stacking the flintlocks inside the stockade, they set the whole U.S. encampment on fire. Leaving the track a wreck, Dibrell led his troops back to the main forces near Spring Creek and told his weary men to sleep until morning.

Nathan Bedford Forrest sent his brother, Jeffrey Forrest, to the south of Jackson with similar instructions, and he captured a garrison of seventy-five men and wrecked the Mobile & Ohio in that direction. Russell's Fourth Alabama and Cox's Tenth Tennessee Cavalry struck the Mississippi Central, burning bridges and culverts. They took fifty prisoners. By morning, Jackson was isolated.[11]

Night, Jackson, Tennessee

Lt. Oliver C. Ayers, Thirty-Ninth Iowa Infantry, had just arrived in Jackson. His regiment was a new unit, just out of a camp where they had received minimum training and then sent south. They were on their way to Corinth when the incursion of Forrest caused their orders to be changed. They stopped in Jackson, Tennessee, to reinforce the garrison there. Ayers kept a journal, and in it he recorded:

> This morning a currier came in telling our Colonel the Rebels were advancing and to be ready. Said the Colonel to the Regiment, they are comeing boys. Just then out through the trees about three fourth of a mile off could be seen a regiment of our men going to meet them. Gracious how our hearts pounded. Only the gleeming of their polished guns could be sen and we mistook them for the Rebels. We expected every minute to be ordered to comence firing but it was soon discovered much to our relief that they were our own men. The Rebs came just close enough so that we could hear the crack of their rifles and commenced to retire. That was plenty close enough though.
>
> We have the pritiest kind of a place to fight behind these

breastworks of cotton. It is almost a pity we could not have had a little scrap but the Duse of it is there would be danger of their giving us more than enough to satisfy our curiosity. Some one I fear will be hurt yet before this is over. There has been considerable fighting around here already. Our Regiment has not happened to get with it yet. Every Cotton bale that is turned over or board that falls down the boys declair it is as Cannon and sometimes we do hear a Cannon in earnest. We are very quiet now awaiting the second approach of the Enemy laying behind our breastworks.

This Morning we were marched out about one half mile and placed behind a long stretch of earth works. Our Regiment were stretched out nearly one half mile. This looks as if there were [too few] troops in here and I guess there was not [enough] this morning. But in spite of the stories about the Rail Roads being torn up several Regiments have arrived here to day.[12]

Friday, December 19, 1862

Yocknapatalfa River Bottoms, Mississippi

The two couriers sent out by Colonel Dickey were happy to see the sky grow brighter. During the night, they had gotten lost. When they finally were able to determine their location, they found that they had traveled in the wrong direction and were further from Oxford and Grant's headquarters than when they had started. It would take them all day and night to reach Oxford, so Grant did not hear the news of the Confederate column passing through Pontotoc until the early morning of December 20.

Near Jackson, Tennessee

The telegraph had gone silent during the night, which meant that Confederates had surrounded the town—or so it seemed. The Union supporters had estimated enemy numbers as high as eight thousand men. During the night, civilians had seen fires on the line of the Mobile & Ohio Railroad both to the north and to the south and on the Mississippi Central to the southwest. All night, a long line of campfires blazed brightly along a ridge about five miles out from the Lexington road. Early on the morning of December 19, a train loaded with wood had been attacked at Carroll Station and received considerable damage. All of these events made Col. Adolph Englemann nervous. He had under his command the Forty-Third and the Sixty-First Illinois infantry regiments as well as parts of the Fifth Ohio, Eleventh Illinois, and Second West Tennessee Cavalry.

The U.S. cavalry units took up a forward position along a ridge overlooking a creek. Forrest had two companies of Woodworth's Regiment, about four hundred men from Biffle's Battalion, and two guns from Freeman's Battery, but they remained mostly hidden in the woods so as to conceal their true numbers. Occasionally, Confederate horsemen rode into the open and fired at the U.S. position at long range, intending to draw return fire and mark the enemy's position. As soon as he knew the Yankee position, Freeman opened guns, and the blue horsemen fell back. This same pattern was repeated several times, until the blue cavalry reached their infantry supports at Salem Cemetery. At this point, the U.S. cavalrymen decided that they had done enough for one day and rode off to Jackson. Most of these men had been overrun by Forrest the day before at Lexington.

The Illinois infantry repelled one probe of its line, but when Forrest sent men around both flanks of their position, Colonel Englemann decided to retreat and retire to Jackson. The colonel felt that he had killed at least sixty Rebels, having lost one man killed and four wounded of his own. In reality, Forrest only lost three men.

The rest of the day, Forrest stayed near Jackson, resting his men. He used all manner of ruses to conceal his numbers from the enemy. Somehow, Forrest had obtained a number of drums usually used by the infantry. He had these beaten at all hours and in various locations to suggest that foot soldiers were part of his force. He ordered details to kindle surplus campfires and to keep them burning all night to make the bivouac appear larger. Knowing that civilians had a way of spreading gossip, even to the Yankees, Forrest encouraged his men to exaggerate his numbers. One recalled, "I heard Trooper Tom Jones talk to an old woman who asked how many men Forrest had. Jones asked if she knew how many trees were between Jackson and the Mississippi River. She said she did not. Jones said he didn't know either but he believed Forrest had enough men to put one behind every tree and two or three behind the really big trees."[1]

Nashville, Tennessee

Rosecrans was not yet worried about cavalry raids. The action on his immediate front was confined to clashes of patrols, the usual condition when major armies confronted each other at close range. His more immediate concern was to alleviate the difficulty of identifying his men at a distance, especially during a battle. In an attempt to solve this problem, Rosecrans ordered each corps in his army to sew a specified identification device on its flag. Each division in each corps was to have the same device but with the addition of a Roman numeral.[2]

On the Road near Ripley, Mississippi

It was a cold morning after a wet night in Mississippi, but Van

Dorn had his men on the road moving north from Ripley at an early hour. A strong rearguard now rode some distance behind the main column, while roving patrols were out on both flanks and in advance. At about mid-morning, the local men guiding Van Dorn revealed an unused and partially overgrown road leading west. They said that the route would be difficult because there were ridges to cross that had swampy areas between them, but it would offer concealment. The proposed route intersected the main Holly Springs-to-Ripley road just a few miles outside of Holly Springs.

By going north beyond Ripley, Van Dorn hoped to mislead the U.S. forces, making it seem that he had bypassed Holly Springs for northern Mississippi in order to strike the Memphis & Charleston Railroad. At about 3:00 p.m., the saddle-weary men were allowed a rest in order to feed their horses and to eat whatever food they had themselves. Many of the men had cold baked sweet potatoes and cold fried bacon. They comforted themselves in hoping that there would be plenty of rations tomorrow. During this break, Van Dorn sent a scout ahead to Holly Springs to make sure that nothing had changed since the last intelligence had been received. He also gave the three brigades in the column their preliminary orders concerning the attack.

Dark came early on December 19, and soon the column groped its way forward, posting guards at every house passed to make sure that no civilian spread word of their arrival.[3]

Oxford, Mississippi

Once Colonel Dickey had reached friendly territory, he left his men under his second in command and rode ahead with a small party to report in person to General Grant. Since Dickey's report was rather routine, Grant listened with little apparent interest—until the colonel mentioned Van Dorn's column at Pontotoc. Grant jumped to his feet and left the room, walking rapidly some four hundred yards to the telegraph office, where he began to send dispatch after dispatch to commanders of garrisons to the north, warning them that a considerable force of Confederate cavalry was on the loose somewhere in northern Mississippi. By this time, the couriers that Dickey had sent had not yet arrived.[4]

Saturday, December 20, 1862

Lumpkin's Plantation, Four Miles South of Holly Springs, Mississippi

It was near 3:00 a.m. when a sentry of the 109th Illinois saw a shadowy figure approaching. When the challenge was issued, the figure halted, and, on being ordered to do so, approached the sentry. The person approaching was a newly freed black man who claimed to have information about a large number of Confederates in the area. The sentry called for the Corporal of the Guard to pass the problem to someone of a higher rank. When the regimental commander, Col. J. Nimmo, was awakened and heard what the man had to say he sent the informant under escort to Col. Robert Murphy, Eighth Wisconsin Infantry, commanding the garrison at Holly Springs.

At about 5:00 a.m., a sleepy Colonel Murphy heard the man's story and gave it very little credit. Still, he sent a telegram to General Grant, passing on the report of five thousand Confederate cavalry fourteen miles east of Holly Springs on the Ripley road. He sent one messenger to the railroad superintendent to prepare two trains to leave for a safer location and dispatched another messenger to the fairgrounds to tell the Second Illinois Cavalry to meet him at the depot at daybreak. Then, Murphy went back to bed.

However, one detail of his report was inaccurate. Van Dorn and his men were not fourteen miles away—they were only fourteen hundred yards.

It was later alleged that Colonel Murphy had been to a Christmas party on the evening of December 19 and that he remained there until the early hours of the December 20. Perhaps this is why he so easily persuaded himself that he was in no imminent danger.[1]

Just Outside of Holly Springs

Van Dorn's spies and scouts provided accurate information.

There were three encampments of U.S. troops in Holly Springs. About one half-mile north of the courthouse, six companies of the 2nd Illinois Cavalry were posted at the fairgrounds. About two hundred men of the 62nd Illinois Infantry were garrisoned around the courthouse square along with small detachments of the 20th, 26th, and 29th Illinois. Five companies of the 101st Illinois were stationed at the depot of the Mississippi Central Railroad.

Van Dorn assigned a different target to each of the brigades in his command. McCulloch's force was to dismount at the edge of town and capture the garrison at the depot. The Texas Brigade was to make for the courthouse square, and, after securing that location, to send regiments to block roads leading into town. The Seventh Tennessee was to move into a blocking position north of Holly Springs. The First Mississippi was to charge into and through town to tackle the Second Illinois Cavalry.[2]

Oxford, Mississippi

It was sometime after midnight when Grant finished sending warnings to his scattered garrisons. He then ordered his cavalry to begin a pursuit as soon as it was light enough to see.

Daybreak, Holly Springs, Mississippi

The column of horsemen had been sitting in their saddles, quietly but impatiently, for some minutes. It was obvious that the first Yankee outpost was only a short distance ahead, but Van Dorn wanted to wait until there was enough light by which to see his opponents; then, a quiet order was given. A participant recalled,

> We moved forward at a trot, soon increased to a gallop, and when a turn in the road brought the pickets in view, they were standing peering at us through the gloom, evidently unable to decide whether we were friend or foe. A stern command from the officer in front to throw down their arms and get out of the road was quickly obeyed, and we passed them like them like the wind. Another turn in the road and the white tents of the camp were in full view.
>
> On a slight eminence near the road side and within gun shot of the camp were three or four horsemen; in passing hem, General van Dorn was recognized in the group and was greeted by a thunderous shout which he gracefully acknowledged and pointed to the enemy with his sword. The charge was instantly turned into a steeple chase and in another moment we struck the camp like a thunderbolt.[3]

The surprise was absolute, and the U.S. soldiers, many still rolled in their blankets, never had a chance to put up any resistance. Although the plan had been for McCulloch's men to dismount to make the attack, the horsemen simply rode down the men emerging from their tents.

The Texas Brigade raced into the courthouse square and found no resistance there either. In a matter of moments, they secured the various billets of men and officers of the occupying force and made the men prisoners. Then the amazed Texans took a look at what they had just captured. They had seen two trains loaded with goods as they raced past the depot and the encampment there. But on the square, there were buildings containing mountains of goods. A livery stable near the courthouse was filled with unopened boxes of pistols and carbines, artillery ammunition filled a nearby brick building, hundreds of bales of cotton lined the streets around the courthouse, other buildings held thousands of rounds of small-arms ammunition, and army rations were stacked under sheds and under tarpaulins. The choice prize was the wagons of the sutlers, rolling emporiums filled with whiskey, wine, cigars, canned oysters, lemons, and luxuries of which the needy Rebs had long dreamed.[4]

The First Mississippi had been tasked with capturing the Second Illinois Cavalry at the fairgrounds, so they paid no attention to the capture of the depot or the spoils on display at the square but rode directly to their objective. At the fairgrounds, the Second Illinois was up, mounted, and in line. They had followed the orders Murphy had sent them earlier that morning to meet him at the depot at daybreak. Not only were they in line, they were ready for a fight. Soon, a hand-to-hand fight swirled across the grassy area. The Mississippi troopers withdrew to the top of a slight hill overlooking the fairgrounds in order to regroup and give their horses a moment to breathe. During this brief interval, some of the Texas troopers from the square who had ridden to the sound of the guns arrived in the rear of the Second Illinois. Caught between two fires, the blue cavalry broke, every man for himself. About 130 escaped, 75 of whom rode all the way to Memphis before they stopped.[5]

S. B. Barron of the Third Texas told a story that illustrated the complexity of the issues of slavery and race during the war. Barron rode the horse of a comrade who had been captured, his own horse having been killed. He decided to acquire a new horse for himself so that he could return his friend's animal when he returned. The challenge was how to lead a spare horse. While puzzling over this problem, he saw a young black man coming out of a side street. Barron asked who he was and what he was doing there. In reply, the young man said his name was Jake and that he had been taken from a plantation on the Tallahatchie River by the Yankees who needed labor at Holly Springs. Jake agreed to travel with Barron and to lead a spare horse. Barron then caught a horse he liked, caught a mule for Jake, and told Jake to follow them when the column left town and to keep asking until he found the camp of Company C, Third Texas. That night, when the regiment bivouacked, Jake showed up riding his mule and leading the horse. Jake stayed with Barron until the end of the war.[6]

As Col. Jack Wharton led the 6th Texas south to guard the road leading to Lumpkin's plantation, several citizens told him that the 109th Illinois was ready and willing to surrender. Several of the officers of the regiment had offered to surrender to a group of Confederate guerrillas a few days before. The major cause of discontent in the unit was the Emancipation Proclamation. Illinois had a law prohibiting black people from residing in the state without first posting a large bond. These men did not like people of color and they had no intention to risk their lives on behalf of people they despised. Wharton considered the information and decided to do nothing. A discontent and inefficient regiment in the U.S. Army was more valuable to the Confederates than a group of men on parole.[7]

As soon as all of the roads leading into town were blocked, the work of destruction began. New arms and equipment were distributed and all available containers were filled with food and ammunition. The rest would have to be destroyed, and that work would be done by fire. In an attempt to avoid a massive explosion of the ammunition, Van Dorn ordered that shells and cartridges be carried into the street and small piles be made of them. Burning these would be less destructive. Although the plan was the best that could be done under the circumstances, it did not work. Fires soon sprang up in several buildings around the square, and a large building being used by the U.S. forces was riddled with shell fragments. Other buildings around the square were also damaged. Amazingly, however, no lives were lost in this process.

Of course, some men could not resist the ready availability of liquor in the sutlers wagons and some men became drunk. Van Dorn, who knew that the success of the expedition required keeping the men in hand, squelched this activity immediately.

The civilian residents of Holly Springs were ecstatic to see the Confederates arrive. Women ran into their yards still wearing their housecoats to welcome "their boys." The men of the town soon made themselves available as sources of information about which houses contained Yankee officers billeted on the residents. Colonel Griffith, commanding the Texas Brigade, was the temporary Provost, whose duty included arresting all the officers he could find. At one house, where several staff officers of Grant's headquarters were staying, the Provost surprisingly found Mrs. Julia Grant. Colonel Boggess ordered ten men to search the house for additional prisoners when Mrs. Grant physically barred the gate. Rather than physically remove her, the detail tore a picket off the fence and went in through the gap. Mrs. Grant then retired to the parlor of the house and stayed there for the rest of the day.[8] The story of the "capture" of Julia Grant has been retold in several secondary accounts of the Holly Springs raid, but all the accounts depend on the record first told by Victor M. Rose in his book. In his account, Rose does not claim to have been an eye-witness to these events, and no other person, on either side, who wrote a first-person account of the raid, mentions Mrs. Grant. Some sources indicate that General Grant had left Holly Springs two or three days earlier and that Mrs. Grant left town the day before the raid.

As daylight began to fade, Van Dorn called in his outposts, formed up his column, and rode out of town. U.S. forces were approaching the southern end of town, but neither side attempted a pursuit.

In a letter to his mother, written after the raiders had returned to their own lines, Lt. James Bates of the Ninth Texas described the personal results of the raid: "I got all I wanted in the way of clothing—a hat, coat, shirts and a pair of cavalry boots—worth here fifty dollars—a fine pair spurs and a horse—also a splendid sash (military)—and sword—the last belonged to a Colonel of cavalry, fresh fruits—pickles, preserves, jams, oysters, Tobacco, cigars &c were strewn by our men all over town."[9]

Outside Oxford, Mississippi

General Grant was furious. He felt that with all of the cotton bales and other supplies available in Holly Springs, an officer with any sense could have constructed temporary breastworks, which would have allowed his men to stand off Van Dorn and any amount of cavalry brought against them. He planned to dismiss Colonel Murphy from the service in disgrace in a matter of hours. This was the second time Murphy had committed a major error. In September 1862 at Iuka, Mississippi, Murphy hastily had abandoned the town, allowing a large amount of military supplies to fall into Confederate hands—even though his sole purpose in being in Iuka was to destroy the material. Grant was also unhappy with his cavalry commanders who had spent most of December 20 in making preparations to ride.

Col. John Mizner, Third Michigan, led the cavalry remaining with Grant once Dickey had been dispatched on his mission. Mizner received Grant's order to be ready to move at daylight on December 20. Instead, he waited for dawn to begin to make preparations for his move. Mizner was a regular army officer and had been in command of the Third Michigan since March 1862. He had several battles under his belt, including Iuka and Corinth, but on this occasion he moved very cautiously. As a result of his dilatory move, his regiment did not reach Oxford on December 20 but bivouacked several miles outside of the town.

Col. Benjamin Grierson also received a telegram from Grant. Grierson was a music teacher from Pittsburgh who had been afraid of horses when the war opened. He was not yet famous, since his spectacular raid through Mississippi would take place in 1863, but he already had made a reputation as a solid commander. He roused his men immediately and was on the road by 1:00 a.m. He waited for Mizner until 6:30 a.m., and, when he did not appear, he moved on to Oxford and reached Grant's headquarters by 1:00 p.m. He spent the rest of the day and part of the next waiting for Mizner.

Having reevaluated his position in light of his colonels' statuses, Grant recognized the utter success that Van Dorn had achieved and ordered his army to retreat.[10]

Spring Creek, Tennessee

At daybreak, Forrest had his men ready to ride. Russell and the Fourth Alabama stayed at the crossing of Spring Creek to delay any pursuit that might have come out of Jackson. During much of the day, Russell played a game of bluff with a force sent out from Jackson, skirmishing and falling back, only to advance again when opportunity offered. At the end of the day, a U.S. force got across Spring Creek, but before it could be reinforced, Russell charged and drove it back to the south side of the stream. In the darkness, Russell abandoned the field, his work having been successfully accomplished.

Forrest sent Dibrell's regiment to capture a stockade guarding the railroad bridge over the Forked Deer River and to burn the bridge. Dibrell marched immediately, taking with him two guns commanded by John Morton. The stockade should have been an easy target, but a brigade of infantry arrived just as Dibrell attacked, and he found himself badly outnumbered. Indeed, he had difficulty extracting himself from the engagement and lost a number of killed and wounded, whom he had to leave behind. Dibrell led his men on to Trenton, the target toward which Forrest had gone.

As Forrest traveled toward Trenton on the Mobile & Ohio Railroad, a town with a small U.S. garrison and a large depot of supplies, he dispatched Col. J. W. Starnes to take care of the Yankees in the town of Humboldt. Starnes caught the defenders unaware of his approach, so he charged them while they were still outside their stockade. The U.S. troops surrendered immediately. Taking what he could carry, Starnes burned the rest of the army goods as well as a trestle on the railroad at Humboldt.[11]

After dispatching these regiments for their various tasks, Forrest sent Biffle to cut off Trenton from the north and east. This left him with his escort of about 100 men and Cox's Battalion of some 200 men to make the attack on Trenton. He did have, in reserve, Freeman's Battery, which would come into play as soon as the enemy position was defined. Col. Jacob Fry commanded the U.S. forces at Trenton (such as they were). When Forrest was first known to have crossed the Tennessee River, all of the smaller posts had been stripped of men to boost the numbers garrisoning Jackson. Now, as Forrest approached, Colonel Fry found he could muster only some 250 men from a dozen or more regiments, most of them men who had been left behind because they were ill. This did not give Fry enough men to man the defenses of the town, so he withdrew his command to the depot.

The depot was not located in a defensible position, being under the brow of a hill some four hundred yards away. Still, Fry barricaded the building with cotton bales and other bulky items and sent thirty-one men into town to serve as sharpshooters from the tops of some buildings.

Forrest led his escort into Trenton at around 3:00 p.m. and dashed through the streets toward the depot, where citizens told him that Fry was ready to make a stand. Under an accurate fire from the U.S. sharpshooters, Forrest split his column, moved around their position out of range, and deployed his own sharpshooters to counter their fire. This sort of combat took on a humanizing approach to the combat for at least one of the men. About one hundred yards from a grocery stood a stimmery, a factory where stems were removed from tobacco leaves before they were sent to market. A Confederate marksman in the tobacco building exchanged ten shots with a U.S. sharpshooter on top of Considine's Grocery. After the Confederate fired his eleventh shot, no fire was returned. When the body was recovered the next day, it was that of Sam Piper, 122nd Illinois Infantry.[12]

While the drama involving the sharpshooters was being played out, Capt. John Strange, the brigade adjutant, brought the guns of Freeman's Battery into position on the hill overlooking the depot. The position was just out of accurate rifle range but provided an easy shot for the cannon. The first shot dislocated a cotton bale from the breastworks protecting the depot, and soon, shots were whizzing through the building itself. With a large amount of ammunition stored in the depot, the defenders were in danger of being blown up by their own supplies. When Forrest sent in a white flag with a demand for unconditional surrender, the U.S. troops immediately accepted. Forrest found himself in possession of two hundred barrels of pork, twenty thousand rounds of artillery ammunition, four hundred thousand rounds of small arms ammunition, and one hundred thousand rations.[13] After making sure his command was supplied, Forrest opened the storehouse to the townspeople.

One of those who helped themselves from the leftovers in the depot was T. Lee Wells. He got for himself a rifle and two good shotguns. On the way back to his house, he passed a local merchant, Robert Seat, who stood on the sidewalk with a two-gallon bucket of beer and several iced ginger cakes, each about a foot square and three inches thick. Wells offered to trade one of the shotguns for all the beer and ginger cake he could consume on the spot. For the rest of his life, Wells contended that he got his money's worth, but he never again had any appetite for beer or ginger cake.

An undocumented story notes that Forrest found among the spoils a saber that caught his fancy. In regulation fashion, the blade was sharp for only six inches from the tip of the blade. Forrest drafted a trooper to turn a grindstone and sat on the porch of a store sharpening the blade for its entire length. When one of his officers told him that sabers normally were sharpened for only a short part of their length, Forrest replied, "Damn such foolishness. War means fighting and fighting means killing. Turn the grindstone." True or not, the story sums up Forrest's military philosophy.

Alexandria, Tennessee

Gen. John Hunt Morgan and his bride, Mattie, arrived in Alexandria. While Mattie settled into the room she and her husband would share for the night, the general met with his officers. Several battalions and companies that had not been assigned to regiments joined the command at Alexandria and were assigned to existing regiments. Then, Morgan organized the entire command into two brigades, one under Col. Basil Wilson Duke and the other under Col. William C. P. Breckinridge.

Basil Wilson Duke was a native of Kentucky and a graduate of Transylvania Law School. He was practicing law in St. Louis when the war began and immediately returned to his home territory to enlist as a private under his brother-in-law, John Hunt Morgan. Duke became a brigadier in September 1864. William Campbell Preston Breckinridge was a cousin of John C. Breckinridge. His father was a staunch Unionist, so the war literally set father against son. Colonel Breckinridge led multiple brigades as the war progressed.[15] Morgan chose subordinates he trusted and who had the necessary experience to handle the task at hand.

Morgan would lead the column north with Duke's Second Kentucky at the head of the line of march commanded by Col. John B. Hutchinson, as Duke had been given other responsibilities. Next in line was the Seventh Kentucky (sometimes called the Third) under Lieutenant Colonel Huffman, its usual commander, the Eighth Kentucky under Col. Leroy Cluke, and Palmer's Georgia Battery of two twelve-pounders and two six-pounders. This gave Duke about twenty-one hundred men. Under Col. William Breckinridge rode Col. Robert G. Stoner's Ninth Kentucky, Col. Adam R. Johnson's Tenth Kentucky, Col. David W. Chenault's Eleventh Kentucky, and Col. James D. Bennett's Fourteenth Tennessee. C. C. Corbett commanded two mountain howitzers and Captain White led a crew with three-inch Parrot rifles to provide artillery support. Breckinridge thus had about eighteen hundred men.

Of the seven colonels commanding these regiments, five became brigade commanders and the other two died soon after the Christmas Raid. During the raid, Colonel Bennett contracted an illness that led to his death in January 1863, and Colonel Chenault was killed in action on July 4, 1863, during the Ohio Raid.[16]

Sunday, December 21, 1862

Davis's Mills, Mississippi

Somebody had finally listened to General Grant. Col. William H. Morgan was in charge of a detachment of his regiment, the Twenty-Fifth Indiana, which had been assigned the responsibility of guarding a bridge of the Mississippi Central Railroad crossing Wolf River at Davis's Mills. As soon as Morgan received word that a raiding force was on its way, he moved his men into an old sawmill that he strengthened with railroad ties and cotton bales. This improvised blockhouse was only seventy yards from the railroad trestle, and it also commanded the only stream crossing in the direction of Holly Springs. About three hundred yards from the blockhouse, on top of an Indian mound, the colonel had his men construct a circular earthwork so as to have a cross-fire on anyone attacking the trestle.[1]

Davis's Mills is some eighteen miles north of Holly Springs, and it was noon before Van Dorn's command arrived. Lieutenant Bates of the Ninth Texas complained that his men, who were the advance guard, "were pushed forward without even knowing where or how the enemy was situated and their strength. This was however only in accordance with Van Dorn's acts generally."[2] The Ninth Texas found that the Yankee position was on the far side of the river and that the flooring had been removed from the bridge. The only ways left to cross the stream were either to run across the stringers of the road bridge or to cross on the ties of the railroad bridge. Neither was feasible under the fire of the defenders.

One of the attackers recalled,

> Running along the bank up the river to the right was a levee some three feet high. The men in front, five or six impetuous fellows, running on to the stringers, one of them fell as he started across, and the others crossed the river. When I reached the bridge the

command was deploying behind the levee without attempting to cross. I remained near the bridge. By this time I was more fatigued, I thought, than I had ever been, with the perspiration streaming off my face, cold as the day was. Here we kept up a fire at the smoke of the enemy's guns as we could not see anything else, until a courier could find General Van Dorn, inform him of the situation and ascertain his wishes as to the advisability of our attempting to cross the river. Anxious to know what had become of the men that went onto the bridge, I rose up and looked over the levee. One of them had been killed and was lying in the edge of the water, and the others were crouched under the opposite bank of the river out of immediate danger. While this observation only required a moment of time and a moment's exposure above the levee, I distinctly felt a minie ball fan my right cheek. While I had not doubted for a moment that I was going to be shot somewhere sometime during the day, this narrow escape of having a minie ball plow through my cheek was very unpleasant . . . I settled down behind the levee and continued firing my Sharp's rifle without exposing myself. Finally we were ordered to fall back.[3]

Since Van Dorn had come equipped to destroy any U.S. installations by fire, someone gave the order to get the bottles of turpentine. The men acquired cotton and soaked the fiber in the oil. These fireballs were then tossed onto and under the trestle, but the heavy rains of the previous days had left the timbers too waterlogged to catch fire. Still, while some men shot at the U.S. defenders, others tore up the track for some distance both above and below Davis's Mills.[4]

A soldier in the Third Texas recorded that "the fight lasted without intermission for about three hours when General Van Dorn, seeing the futility of his attacks on the fortified position without guns called off the men . . . A Confederate hospital was established on the field and left in charge of Assistant-Surgeon Eugene Blocker of the 3rd Texas."[5] Van Dorn, who had never led a cavalry raid before, had just learned a bloody lesson that Forrest and Morgan had learned much earlier: artillery might be slow and need to be double-teamed, but it was invaluable against positions that had any degree of fortification. Forrest would have had a difficult—if not impossible—task in capturing Trenton had he not had Freeman's Battery with him. If the buildings around the courthouse square in Holly Springs had been barricaded, Van Dorn would have failed in his mission there. Even a section of six-pounders would have brought about the surrender of the Davis's Mills garrison. Van Dorn encountered the same problem later in this raid, as well. As it was, he needlessly lost both men and time. "Private George Stringfellow of Company H had advanced in front of the company and a Yankee sharpshooter shot him through the head. Though his comrades knew that Stringfellow had 5 or 600 dollars in his pocket his position was so exposed that none would dare venture to him." Over several hours of fighting, Van Dorn lost twenty-two dead and thirty wounded and achieved the same result as had he simply surrounded the blockhouse at a distance while his track wreckers were at work.[6]

The Confederates had seen quite enough of Davis's Mills and were glad to hear the bugle sound "recall" and to ride away. The Indiana men were proud of the defense they had made, but they, too, were happy to see Van Dorn leave.

Near Nashville on Wilson's Creek Pike

Wheeler had made life so difficult for Rosecrans's foraging parties that they now had to be guarded by large details. Companies A and B of the Fourth Michigan Cavalry were called out to assist a foraging party that had gone down the Franklin Pike to the fork with Wilson's Creek Pike and had then followed that road. The foragers were already protected by two regiments of infantry, a section of artillery, and part of the Fifth Kentucky Cavalry (U.S.). The Kentucky troops engaged in a brisk skirmish with a party of Confederate cavalrymen that had positioned itself behind one of the many stone walls that crossed the fields and pastures of Middle Tennessee. The Fourth Michigan had superior firepower, being armed with Colt five-shot revolving rifles. Their commander dismounted his men and advanced on foot, but even the revolving rifles were no match for men well-protected behind a stone wall. A mounted charge covered the distance to the wall quickly so that the Confederates could not pour in enough fire to stop it.

The foraging party was able to get back to Nashville, but at a great expense of manpower and effort. Wheeler was doing all he could to keep the Army of the Cumberland shut up in Nashville.[7]

Trenton, Tennessee

Forrest took the morning to reorganize and resupply his command. The scattered regiments that had been sent on separate duties were concentrated at Trenton, and Forrest issued the captured weapons and supplies to his men. Col. Dibrell reported that the Eighth Tennessee "participated in the divide of the large amount of supplies captured by the general at Trenton, and there finished equipping the regiment with good guns, clothing, &c."[8] The Eighth had crossed the Tennessee River only a few days before with more than four hundred of its men carrying flintlocks. Clearly, Forrest was doing well for the men under his command.

Forrest left Dibrell at Trenton to guard the road leading toward Jackson while the rest of the command took roads leading toward Union City. He ordered the commissary wagons under Maj. G. V. Rambaut along a route thought to be quite safe. Accompanying the train were a few men whose horses had gone lame and who could not keep up with the mounted column. Much to the surprise of the major, when the column came in sight of Rutherford Station, the U.S. flag was still flying over a small stockade there. Why the garrison had not been evacuated was a mystery to all, but Rambaut took full advantage of a rare opportunity for a rear echelon staff officer. He told the men on the lame horses to dismount and to surround the place. Soon enough, they fired shots to keep the nervous garrison pinned below the parapet of their stockade. Having "treed the critter," Rambaut was at something of a loss as to what to do next. Then, Forrest, his Escort Company, and two of Freeman's guns came up the road. With artillery now in position, the U.S. troops took the path of wisdom and surrendered. Not every day did a commissary officer take 250 prisoners.[9]

The Confederate column followed the railroad to Kenton Station, wrecking the track as they went. At Kenton Station, the 119th Illinois was in a stockade, but a brief bombardment from Freeman's guns caused them to raise a white flag. Here, the railroad crossed the Obion River on a long trestle, so Forrest ordered his command to stop for the day, allowing plenty of time to destroy the structure.[10]

Alexandria, Tennessee

Lt. John Porter of the Ninth Kentucky knew that something big was about to happen. General Morgan had rejoined his command, new units had been integrated into existing regiments, and horses and weapons had been inspected. As the sun passed its zenith, the bugles sounded "assembly," and from the various hollows around Alexandria, the regiments gathered on a large field. There, Morgan read a General Order that informed the men that they were about to start on a difficult and dangerous mission—to conquer Kentucky. Many men spent much of the night making preparations for the ride.[11]

One man not preparing for the mission was Morgan's adjutant, Col. St. Leger Grenfell. It appears that this soldier of fortune thought that he should have been given command of the second of Morgan's ad hoc brigades, and, rather than serve under Breckinridge or Duke, he took his leave, riding back to Murfreesboro to ask Bragg for another assignment.[12]

On the Road from Oxford to Holly Springs, Mississippi

Grant's men were hungry. The army had been placed on half-rations as soon as they heard about the destruction of Holly Springs. Grant had thought to supplement his rations by foraging, but that would not have been very effective. The Army of Tennessee had passed through the region and had left little behind. Some Illinois regiments were issued a single hardtack cracker as the entire day's ration, while others recalled marching for two days with almost nothing to eat. The memory of hunger was universal in the accounts of those who made the retreat from Mississippi to Memphis.[13]

Jackson, Tennessee

Gen. Sullivan was not having much success in his pursuit of Forrest. He had chased but had not apprehended; indeed, the only result of his search was that men of his command had gotten gobbled up. Lt. Ayers recorded in his journal:

> The expedition which has been out under General Sulivan the Commander of this District came in today having chaced the Rebels across the Tennessee River or a part of them it seems, for while he was at this a force went up the Rail Road to Trenton and Humbolt, places between here and Columbus, and captured our forces at each of these places which had been weakened to reinforce this place. We started North on the Rail Road toward these places. About ten miles from here we found a bridge burned. Our Company was detailed to guard the train back to this place and so here we are while the rest of our Regiment is with one or two others at the Burned Bridge which they are mending."[14]

Monday, December 22, 1862

Kenton Station, Tennessee

For fifteen miles beyond Kenton, the Mobile & Ohio ran over trestles that carried the rails across the swampy bottoms of the Obion River, an area that flooded from winter until well into summer. Forrest put the larger part of his command to work destroying these wooden structures. Among the spoils of war taken at Trenton were five hundred axes, and these were now put to use. The country boys who made up the bulk of Forrest's command soon discovered an easy way to do the work. They took their axes and began to split kindling. Soon, large bonfires blazed at regular intervals along the trestles, catching the woodworks aflame and sending large sections crashing into the muck below.[1]

Alexandria, Tennessee

It was still early in the day when a carriage came in sight of the thirty-nine hundred men assembled in an open field at Alexandria. Behind the carriage rode a uniformed orderly leading a horse, which many of the soldiers identified as belonging to General Morgan. As the carriage came to the assembled men, it stopped, and both the general and Mattie got out. The two took a brief goodbye, and then Morgan mounted his horse and gave the order to forward march. One of the men in the ranks recalled that two batteries, totaling seven pieces of artillery, accompanied the men. There were four hundred unarmed men who would serve as horse-holders until they could acquire weapons. No one carried a saber, but most of the men who had been in service at least a year had one or two Colt Navy model .36 pistols. Some of the men had carbines, and many had double-barrel shotguns—a fearsome weapon at close range. Most of the command carried rifles. Every man had three days' cooked rations, sixty rounds of ammunition, two horseshoes, twelve horseshoe nails, a blanket, and either an oil cloth poncho or an overcoat. Except for the double-teamed artillery, there was nothing on wheels.[2]

A good road led from Alexandria toward the Cumberland River, and the column made good time despite the recent heavy rains. By the end of the first day, part of the command had crossed the river at Sand Shoals, near Carthage, Tennessee, and the rest were closed up on the south bank, ready to cross in the morning.[3]

Locks Mill, Tennessee

Van Dorn had reached the point where the Memphis & Charleston Railroad became his target. This rail led from Memphis along the state line of Mississippi and Tennessee, passing through Grand Junction, where it crossed the Mississippi Central. The town of Grand Junction was too heavily garrisoned for any attempt on taking it to have any chance of success, so Van Dorn struck at Locks Mill. His men destroyed a trestle and several hundred yards of track on each side of the stream crossing. Now, Grant's supply line again had been cut, this time even further to his rear. Van Dorn's men were becoming experts in ripping up rails, piling ties, and setting the piles on fire so as to twist and warp the iron rails. They also severely frightened Lt. Col. John McDermott, the U.S. garrison commander at Grand Junction. Before his telegraph went silent as Confederates cut the wires, he reported to Memphis that Van Dorn was preparing to attack him with ten thousand men. He also mentioned several other targets in the dispatch, most of them far from Van Dorn's actual line of march.

Somerville, Tennessee

Leaving the wrecked Memphis & Charleston, Van Dorn moved on toward Somerville, Tennessee. As the men rode into town, they found a mass meeting going on, the purpose of which was to whip up support for the Union and to select Union men for political office. This was part of Lincoln's plan to reconstruct seceded states in which significant areas had been occupied by the U.S. Army. Everyone in Van Dorn's column wore a blue overcoat, captured at Holly Springs, and cased their flags. The men mingled freely with the pro-Union crowd for some time. When the citizens suddenly realized that their "guests" might not appreciate the sentiment of the meeting, they abruptly adjourned the proceedings, and ladies with Confederate sympathies appeared with food in their hands.

Some of these, no doubt, had a sudden change of heart! Enjoying a good laugh as well as something good to eat, the men rode seven miles out of town toward Jackson, Tennessee.[4]

Oxford, Mississippi

General Grant was frustrated. His commander at Memphis had reported that Van Dorn had sent in a flag of truce demanding the surrender of the town, and Gen. Samuel R. Curtis, commander of U.S. forces at Memphis, was spending all of his time making sure that government supplies and captured cotton were safe from Confederate hands. It was later learned that this flag had been sent by the leader of a small band of guerrillas, but their demand paralyzed the garrison at Memphis. Except for the men actually shot, it seemed that no one knew where Van Dorn was. So Grant ordered the Twenty-Third Michigan Cavalry to go to Grand Junction and on to Bolivar, reestablishing any posts that had been abandoned. A division of infantry had reached Holly Springs—a classic case of locking the barn door after the equine had gone. Col. Benjamin Grierson wanted to cut loose from the infantry at Holly Springs and go after Van Dorn, and Grant approved the idea and ordered him to do so.[5]

Humboldt, Tennessee

The pursuit of Forrest was not going well. Gen. J. N. Haynie had outrun his supplies as he reached Humboldt, and Forrest had left nothing behind to eat. So, Haynie sent his men out foraging. Lt. Ayers proved to be skillful at the activity of taking food from civilians. He noted in his journal:

> Our Company did its first foraging. We had nothing to eat nor had we for twenty four hours and could not go into town to get any not being allowed to leave our Post. Hearing that the forces in town had to forage for Provision we were soon supplied with plenty of fresh meat, chickens, and corn meal from the neighboring Secesh Citizens telling them they could get pay for the same off Uncle Sam. That is, if they are Loyal Citizens. The fact is, their class cut the Rail Road between us and our supplies leaving us no means of getting Provisions except to Forage off the country. To get pay for this Forage it was necessary for them to show that they are not traitorous to the Government.
>
> At sundown yesterday we went into the fort at Humboldt. Of all nights we ever spent last night was the Chief. I think the men

whose Rest had been so often disturbed had spread their blankets and went to sleep as it was fairly dark. But scarcely had we closed our eyes when bang, bang went the guns of the sentinels. Guns just on the works of the fort under the impression that the Secesh were attacking us. We were in line of battle in less time than it takes me to write it. Here we remained about an hour when we were again ordered to retire. But before half of us were fairly in bed, Guns we heard in the Picket lines and we reluctantly obeyed the order to fall in . . . again we returned to our blankets but not to sleep for again we were called into line and thus it was all night. Not a Picket could fire at a roaming Porker but we must be called into line.[6]

Tuesday, December 23, 1862

Kenton Station, Tennessee

Forrest had taken part of the morning to organize some 450 recruits who had joined his ranks since he entered West Tennessee. He did not plan to send these inexperienced newcomers into battle but to use them as horse-holders and as guards for prisoners of war instead. The number of Forrest's prisoners was becoming unwieldy, so he also spent time having his adjutant make a list of the men and their units and then issue them parole to go home until exchanged. The paroled prisoners were to march as a unit as far as Columbus, Kentucky, where they would report to the commander of the U.S. garrison. As these men assembled with their small escort for the trip north, Forrest, still in their presence, gave orders in a loud voice to a number of couriers, who were to take messages to Colonels So-and-So to bring his unit to meet Forrest at a designated location. These units did not exist, but Forrest knew that the prisoners would relate what they had heard to the commander at Columbus.

Union City, Tennessee

Capt. Samuel Logan, Fifty-Fourth Illinois, was not very happy. General Davies at Columbus had ordered him to take his company to Union City, where the Memphis & Ohio Railroad crossed the Mobile & Ohio Railroad. On arriving at 3:00 p.m., Logan sent out pickets and then allowed his men to cook a meal, since they had not eaten all day. Then the Confederates appeared.

According to Logan's account, a flag of truce accompanying the prisoners of war came up to Logan's position, and the Confederate lieutenant colonel in charge of the escort began negotiations to have the men sent on to Columbus. While these talks were proceeding, Forrest arrived with the bulk of his command, took advantage of the flag of truce, and surrounded Logan's position, demanding the

79

surrender of the company. According to Confederate accounts, the advance guard of Forrest's column came up to Union City and immediately sent in a demand for the surrender of the U.S. troops. While Logan was making up his mind, the prisoners of war approached, and Logan mistook them for Confederates. Seeing that he was outnumbered, he chose to surrender. No matter whose account, the result was the same. Forrest had artillery and outnumbered Logan several times over.[1] No matter how many flags of truce might have been visible, Logan became a prisoner of war. Forrest's men were pleased that not a shot had been fired.

Nolensville, Tennessee

Gen. John Wharton was pleased with his day's work. Earlier that day, he had sent out a patrol made up of detachments from the Eighth Texas (Terry's Texas Rangers) and the Second Georgia. These men had served together since the summer of 1862 and had formed a close working relationship. The patrol had overrun the advance picket protecting the approach to the U.S. lines and, with the picket out of the way, had been able to make a reconnaissance of the advancing U.S. infantry. The army corps of Gen. George Thomas had advanced from Nashville on the Charlotte and Granny White Pikes and had gone into camp there. Wharton had so hindered U.S. foragers that Thomas only sent out parties accompanied by very heavy supports. Not only had Wharton's men brought back prisoners, but also, they had no losses of their own. Wharton dispatched a courier to General Wheeler's headquarters with the news.[2]

Tompkinsville, Kentucky

Morgan's men were cold, tired, and ecstatic. Earlier in the day, they had crossed the state line and had entered Kentucky. For most of the men, this was home. No enemy yet had been seen.[3]

Darcyville, Tennessee

Before leaving on the raid, Van Dorn had entertained the vague idea that he might continue north across Tennessee and join the forces under Forrest. Now, that seemed impossible. Forrest was too far north, and there were too many Yankee forces beginning to take the field looking for him. Van Dorn was sure that U.S. forces must be somewhere on his trail, too. He had confirmed that the town of Bolivar held a well-fortified garrison. He did not have the time or the manpower to attack this position, but he needed to keep the U.S. in their earthworks and not out on his trail. He had led his men to Darcyville the night before to give the impression that he might still be headed for Forrest, but then he turned east and south so as to approach Bolivar from an unexpected direction. His plan worked perfectly, and while his enemies wondered where he was, Van Dorn's men wrecked trestles and bridges both north and south of Bolivar.[4]

Wednesday, December 24, 1862

Jackson, Tennessee

Gen. Jeremiah C. Sullivan did not know just where Nathan Bedford Forrest was, but he believed him to be just out of sight, hidden in the woods or behind ridges, near the fortifications of Jackson. Officially, Sullivan professed himself to be concerned with preventing the captures of the valuable military supplies in Jackson. In reality, he was content to leave Forrest alone so long as Forrest did not attack him. He did not send any strong bodies of troops north from Jackson to probe into the area where Forrest was busy working on the railroad.

Columbus, Kentucky

The telegraph lines south to Grant's headquarters were dead, cut in numerous places by Confederate raiders and the guerrillas who seized the opportunity created by the presence of organized Confederate forces to become more bold in their harassment of U.S. positions.

Gen. Thomas D. Davies, unable to communicate with Grant, his direct superior officer, instead sent a telegram to the department commander, Henry Halleck, in St. Louis. Davies reported that all of the military supplies on hand were being sent to Memphis, that he needed reinforcements to hold Columbus against Forrest's seven thousand cavalry and supporting infantry, and that he believed that Island Number Ten would fall to the Confederates, so he ordered the ammunition stored there to be thrown into the Mississippi River and the twenty-four heavy cannon to be spiked.

From St. Louis, Gen. Henry Halleck issued an order canceling the elections that were to be held to select members of the U.S. Congress from West Tennessee. Reconstruction would have to wait.

Union City, Tennessee

Forrest knew that his enemies would not be long in getting over their initial fears, and he was determined to take full advantage of the time he had. All day on Christmas Eve, his men worked to wreck the bridges that led across the swampy, flooded bottoms of the Obion River. By the end of the day, they had put out of commission some fifteen miles of trestle work and track.

Glasgow, Kentucky

General Morgan was nearing the first town of any consequence he had approached in Kentucky. Following standard military practice, he sent a patrol of men from the Ninth Kentucky and from Quirk's Scouts to determine if there were U.S. troops nearby. As the Confederates rode in from one end of town, a detachment of the Second Michigan Cavalry rode in from the opposite direction. Suddenly, a swirl of combat erupted in the streets as the surprised men on both sides reached for their weapons. In a few minutes, the clash was over, with two Confederates dead and one U.S. soldier dead and another wounded. One of the dead was Confederate 1st Lt. Samuel Peyton, who had been surrounded by several Yankees and shot in the arm and thigh. Despite his wounds, Peyton wrestled one of his attackers from the saddle and cut his throat with a pocket knife before bleeding to death himself. Twenty of the Michigan troopers became prisoners of war, and the Confederates took trophies and spoils, including "a number of Christmas turkeys which the Michigan men had strapped to their saddles."[1]

Middleburg, Tennessee

Finally, the inevitable had occurred. After having ridden so far with minimum pressure, Van Dorn found himself pressed by pursuers. As his men had ridden around Bolivar destroying the railroad, U.S. cavalry had approached. Now, they were hot on his tracks. Just when he needed to move quickly in order to evade the pursuers, Van Dorn came up against another of those hastily fortified positions that were impervious without the artillery he had decided not to bring with him.

U.S. Col. William Graves, Twelfth Michigan, had men scattered all over the area between Middleburg and Bolivar. As a result, there were only 115 present on duty at the village. At 10:30 a.m., an officer went out on a mounted patrol and soon returned with the news that Confederates were approaching. Graves sent out a few skirmishers and led his men into a brick church where the windows had already been barricaded and loopholes cut in the walls. Van Dorn's Texas Brigade sent in a flag of truce with the demand to surrender, a demand that Graves promptly refused.

For the next two and a half hours, Graves's men and Van Dorn's Texas Brigade fought a brisk skirmish around the house of worship, with the Texas troops getting the worst of it. They made repeated attempts to rush the building and to batter in the doors, but the riflemen protected inside drove back each attempt. In the Third Texas, U.S. bullets killed Lt. William Logan, a former law student, along with Ed Lewis and Alva Box. In all, nine men were killed and eleven wounded so badly that they had to be left on the field. The only success Van Dorn had at Middleburg was to loot the abandoned U.S. camp of limited supplies of food and equipment.[2] They left the railroad trestle on the Mississippi Central undamaged.

Bolivar, Tennessee

Col. Benjamin Grierson was ready to fight. He had ridden from Oxford to Holly Springs to Bolivar and had never had a clear idea of just where Van Dorn's men were. Now he knew—they were just seven miles away at Middleburg. "Boots and Saddles" sounded in the camps of the Sixth Illinois and the Seventh Kansas Cavalries, and Grierson took to the road. Grant considered him to be one of, if not the, best cavalry officers under his command.[3]

Van Dorn had made a feint toward Bolivar during the night of December 23, and this had convinced the U.S. commander there to concentrate his forces inside the town's fortifications, expecting an attack. During the night, the main column of Confederates circled around the town and rode on to Middleburg, where the Texas Brigade was already engaged.

Middleburg, Tennessee

Gen. Van Dorn saw no reason to continue the skirmish with the Twelfth Michigan, so he led his men on the road toward Saulsbury and Grand Junction. Soon, his rear guard sent word that Grierson was in sight and coming on fast. Passing through Van Buren, Tennessee, the raiders took time to demolish the trestle on the railroad before pushing on to Saulsbury, which they reached at dark. At this point, Van Dorn was only a mile ahead of his pursuers.

Moving on a little farther, Van Dorn halted his command and allowed the men to build fires.

The U.S. pursuit was close behind, but the overall efforts to catch Van Dorn were confused. This disarray was due, in large part, to the destruction of the telegraph lines wrought by both the main Confederate column and by numerous bands of guerrillas who had taken advantage of the chaos Van Dorn had created. In addition, Col. Albert D. Lee and Col. John K. Mizner were not as enthusiastic in their wish to catch Van Dorn as was Grierson. Mizner was senior in rank to Grierson, and, when he joined Grierson's force, took command of the chase and directed it to his own goals. Ultimately, Grant did not have enough cavalry to mount an effective pursuit of Van Dorn and simultaneously block the routes returning to Confederate territory, so he tried to remedy this lack by dispatching infantry to points where Van Dorn might appear. Of course, the Gray horsemen readily avoided these positions.[4]

Thursday, December 25, 1862

From Kentucky to Tennessee to Mississippi, Christmas Day of 1862 was a memorable holiday.

Union City, Tennessee

Forrest received news from his scouts and informers that a strong force, estimated at ten thousand men, was moving northward to cut off his retreat, but this news did not distract him from the work at hand. By nightfall on December 24, the detachments sent out on various stretches of the Mobile & Ohio had all returned whistling "I've Been Working on the Railroad." So complete had the men done their work that Forrest took advantage of the season to declare Christmas Day a holiday. This did not so much reflect religious sentiment as it was a recognition that his men were worn down to a nub and needed the rest.

Capt. Charles Anderson served as assistant adjutant to Forrest. He knew something about railroads, having been a vice president of the Nashville & Charleston prior to the war. He wrote home about the Christmas festivities of Forrest's men:

> Now the boys lie or stroll about the camp, chewing and smoking, drinking the good coffee they have captured, telling over their deeds, looking for lost buddies, and laying before the big fires. Some have jabbed their ramrods into hunks of dough, made up on the backs of their oilcloth coats, and are holding them before the fire to cook. Others have mixed cornmeal, a pinch of salt, and a little water, wrapped corn shucks about it and are burying it in the hot coals and ashes. A squad is guffawing over the tale of an old woman who complained that "Mr. Forrest and his hoss critters formed a streak of fight in my back yard, tore down my fence, and plumb ruint my ash-hopper." Somebody else, having nothing better to do, cackles like a hen. One of the critters says 'shoo.' Other hens cackle, and others shoo. This grows until the camp sounds like a poultry yard stired up over a mink or a weasel.[1]

Columbus, Kentucky

Gen. Thomas Davis was feeling more confident on Christmas Day. Having ordered the heavy guns at Island Number Ten spiked, he had just learned that all of the sick men at the post and most of the remaining supplies were being loaded on boats and would soon be moving down the Mississippi toward Memphis and safety. This evacuation would enable him to make a much better defense with his able-bodied men. Davis reported that Forrest had seven thousand men at Union City and that reinforcements were likely on the way.

News from Holly Springs reached Davis in the early afternoon, and he forwarded the report to Gen. Henry Halleck in St. Louis. By late evening, Davis was confident that he could hold his position at Columbus, especially since three gun boats had arrived and the Navy had provided him with a number of howitzers to bolster his defenses.[2]

Approaching Green River, Kentucky

Quirk's Scouts led the way for Morgan as he left Glasgow and proceeded up the Bear Wallow Pike toward Munfordville. As the Scouts topped a hill, one of their vedettes halted them to report a line of U.S. cavalry in battle position about a mile ahead. The Scouts made the top of another rise and started down between high rail fences on each side. Suddenly, the hidden Northern cavalry opened fire, and the Scouts took cover in the corners of the fence. A company of the Fifth Indiana charged out of a hidden location and caught the Scouts in the flank and rear. This move stampeded the horses and horse-holders, so the Scouts found themselves in a tight place indeed. U.S. soldiers captured five members of the company, and the rest scrambled over the fence and ran for a thicket of trees some two hundred yards away. Just then, the lead regiment of the main column of Morgan's command came on the scene and saved the Scouts from too rough a handling.[3]

John Porter of the Ninth Kentucky also remembered Christmas Day of 1862. His regiment marched at the rear of Morgan's command, and he was placed in charge of the rear vedette, riding some distance behind the larger rearguard. This arrangement allowed Porter to make occasional discrete pauses at houses of friends and relatives along the way. On one of these stops, at a crossroads, Porter was ordered to remain behind for some time to guard against a possible U.S. move along one of the roads. When the threat did not materialize, he led his men on after the main Confederate column. While doing, so they overtook an immense sutler's wagon, "the largest I ever saw. Who does not remember that wagon? It was full of everything although we were in the extreme rear and four thousand men had gone for it. We had an abundance of everything left for us to eat and to smoke and to drink. This wagon was captured in front of the residence of G. W. Blakely."[4]

Gallatin, Tennessee

Col. John Harlan commanded the Second Brigade of Cavalry under Rosecrans. Late on Christmas night, he received orders to move his men by rail to Bowling Green, Kentucky, and on to Cave City. The news of Morgan's raid had at last reached Rosecrans, and he finally was taking action—or at least ordering it.

Harlan, a future Justice of the U.S. Supreme Court, was an attorney in Louisville when the war began. He had graduated from Centre College and Transylvania University Law School, where he had been a classmate of Basil Wilson Duke.

Harlan faced one frustration after another. The order to Harlan stated that engines and cars from Nashville would reach him sometime very early on December 26, so he immediately began to assemble his command: five regimens of infantry and a battery of artillery. No long, winter's nap was in store for the Gallatin's U.S. garrison.[5]

Nashville, Tennessee

Gen. William S. Rosecrans made his headquarters at 13 High Street, the residence of the George Cunningham family. On Christmas night, he held a lengthy council of war in a bedroom that had been transformed into an office. All the division and corps commanders were present, and it was midnight before they reached any conclusion.

Gen. William Rosecrans issued orders for the Army of the Cumberland to move toward Murfreesboro the next morning at 6:00 a.m., about as early as there would be light enough to see.[6]

Saulsbury, Tennessee

Morning came early for the Confederates, not because they expected a visit from St. Nicholas, but because they wished to avoid a visit from Grierson. At 1:00 a.m., Van Dorn ordered his men awakened, and soon afterward they took the road toward Ripley, Mississippi. He left a detail behind to keep the campfires burning, but this ruse was of limited effect. Grierson's scouts told him at 2:00 a.m. that the Confederates were moving out. More effective was Van Dorn's use of guides, men in his ranks who had grown up in the area and local residents who were glad to assist the war effort. With this aid showing him shortcuts and local roads, Van Dorn made good time to Ripley, east of Holly Springs. Delayed by poor communications and a lack of desire on the part of Col. Albert Lee and Mizner, it was well after daybreak before the U.S. pursuit resumed.[7]

Christmas dinner for the Johnny Rebs with Van Dorn consisted of parched corn eaten in the streets of Ripley. A short break was all the men and horses received, as Grierson soon appeared. Van Dorn was ready with a plan of escape. He detailed the Ninth Texas to fight a rearguard action, while the main force moved on, out of sight of their pursuers, in the direction of Grenada. A short distance outside of Ripley, the Confederate command turned into a narrow country road and was soon lost to Grierson's sight.

The Ninth Texas formed a line and began a brisk skirmish with the U.S. force. The Texans fought so hard that Grierson thought that he confronted all of Van Dorn's men with Van Dorn in personal command. Three times the Texas regiment formed a line, and three times they fell back before being brought to close combat. The Union force followed the Texans, but they pursued the wrong road—Van Dorn was leading his men to safety along seldom-used byways. Darkness fell with the running battle still going on, but the main Southern force was getting closer and closer to safety.[8]

Confederate Picket Line, near Nolensville, Tennessee

As usual, the Commissary Department had left something to be desired in the way of rations for Christmas dinner, and, as usual, the cavalry was looking after itself. Lieutenant Bowling, Company D, Fifty-First Alabama, was sent out in command of the pickets. After he had gone, some of the men left in camp tore down an old farm shed for firewood and, in the process, killed a number of very large rats. A private in the shed demolition detail skinned several of the largest rats and wrapped them in wet corn shucks to cook.

When a relief party was sent out to the picket post, the private was included and took his rats with him. Approaching Lt. Bowling, he asked permission to retire to a gully on the reverse side of the hill where they were stationed, build a fire, and roast the "nice young squirrels" he had shot that morning. In return for this permission, he offered to share his bounty of fresh meat. The lieutenant agreed and mightily enjoyed his Christmas dinner. Days later, when he found out what he had been served, he said that he seriously considered shooting the private, except that gun powder was too scarce![9]

Humboldt, Tennessee

Lt. Ayers noted, "We slept undisturbed last night though we had but the cold ground to lie upon. I am fully satisfied that Soldering is no childs play."[10]

Friday, December 26, 1862

Johnson's Plantation, near Chicakasaw Bluffs, Mississippi

William T. Sherman was glad to have his men off of the boats on which they had been confined since December 20. Obeying orders, he had led four divisions from Memphis down the Mississippi to the Yazoo River, from which point he could attack Vicksburg from the northeast. Somewhere to the east, the army under General Grant was supposed to be approaching, although Sherman had heard nothing from Grant since he boarded his men onto the boats.

The Mississippi Delta along the Yazoo River was not an appealing place to conduct a military operation. Thickets of trees and cane, slow-moving streams, and extensive swampy land that quickly flooded in winter rains all made the area difficult to move through. Yet, if Sherman could get a foothold on the Walnut Hills, sometimes called the Chickasaw Bluffs, he would have a good chance of opening the door to Vicksburg once Grant arrived with the rest of the army.

Thanks to the U.S. Navy, the Yazoo had been cleared of Confederate mines, and the transport boats could steam twelve miles up the river, closer to their destination. The landing would be protected by fire from the heavy guns on the boats. Now, Sherman had four divisions either on shore or on their way up the Yazoo.[1]

Gallatin, Tennessee

Col. John Harlan was furious because the trains assigned to carry his men in pursuit of Morgan were completely stationary. Having roused his men on Christmas night so as to be ready for an early start, Harlan had them all aboard the train cars the next morning. The number of cars was minimal (three trains of ten cars each) and all available space was packed with men, weapons, supplies, and horses for the battery accompanying his pursuit expedition. Each train was equipped with a single engine, an arrangement that would soon fail.

93

Harlan had made only six miles and was approaching the South Tunnel on the Louisville & Nashville Railroad when the engine of the rear train broke down. No additional engines were available in Gallatin, so Harlan ordered a telegraph message sent to Nashville. The men aboard simply waited for a replacement to arrive. A passenger train from Nashville bound for Louisville did come along, but the conductor refused to allow his engine to be detached to push the troop train to its destination. Instead, the passenger train backed up to Nashville to clear the track.

The recent rain coupled with the constant track wrecking practiced by guerrillas had left the track in poor condition, so that even when the replacement engine did arrive, it took until 10:00 p.m. for Harlan's men to arrive in Bowling Green.[2] At this rate, it was obvious that this could not be considered a pursuit of Morgan; it was simply the positioning of troops in the hope that Morgan would run into them. Infantry and artillery aboard slow trains or on an even slower march had no hope of catching a cavalry column.

Dresden, Tennessee

Forrest was well aware that it was time to head home. After a day of rest for most of his command, his scouts and friendly civilians had brought news of a closing ring of troops anxious to bag the bold intruder who was so deep in U.S. occupied territory. In all, some twenty thousand U.S. soldiers were fixed in place because of Forrest, and Grant, Sherman, or Rosecrans could have put these men to a better military purpose had they been available.

The most immediate threat came from Jackson, Tennessee, where General Sullivan finally moved with two infantry brigades to block Forrest on his way back south. The infantry could not catch Forrest, but, in the flooded land of West Tennessee, they could occupy strategic river crossings and prevent an escape until more men arrived. Forrest decided to thwart this move by taking his command toward Dresden. Late in the afternoon of December 26, the U.S. garrison at Dresden became prisoners of war, and Forrest burned yet another section of the railroad. Biffle's regiment was sent toward Trenton to guard against surprise, while John Morton took care administrative duties.

A battalion of cavalry under Col. Thomas Alonzo Napier had joined Forrest during the course of the raid, and this unit had in its possession two mountain howitzers. Forrest ordered these two guns to report to Morton, giving him a total of four guns.

Morton organized his battery, which contained sixty-three non-commissioned officers and men. Lt. W. A. Gould commanded one section, and Lt. T. Sanders Sale, the second. Morton was now the youngest artillery captain in all of the Confederate armies.[3]

Nashville, Tennessee

The Yankees were on the move! General Rosecrans had given orders that, at daybreak, the Army of the Cumberland would advance in three wings. Major General McCook took the right wing of three divisions along the Nolensville Pike to Triune. Maj. Gen. George Henry Thomas took the center wing of two divisions down the Franklin and Wilson Pikes and then turn cross-country to Triune. Maj. Gen. Thomas L. Crittenden moved with the left wing directly on Murfreesboro by the pike of that name. Rosecrans had forty-two hundred cavalry under Col. John Kennett, who screened the move. The First Brigade, under Col. Robert H. G. Minty, led Crittenden's advance. The Second Brigade, under Col. Lewis Zahm, covered McCook's right flank by moving on Franklin. Gen. David Stanley, with the title of chief of cavalry, directly commanded a reserve force that would protect the advance down the Nolensville Pike. The infantry took up their march about two hours before the cavalry broke camp, so the horsemen at first found themselves behind the men they were supposed to screen. It took some time to correct this placement in the line of march. Skirmishing broke out across the Union front as the men soon ran into Wheeler's and Wharton's pickets.[4]

Robert Horatio George Minty was born in Ireland but immigrated to Canada and then to Michigan. Minty had served in the Royal Army as an ensign and used that military experience in his Civil War career. He was lieutenant colonel of the Third Michigan before being promoted to colonel to command the Fourth Michigan. He became a brigadier in March 1863.

Lewis Zahm was born in Ziebruchen, Germany, in 1820. He came to the U.S. following the 1848 revolution and was living in Ohio when commissioned to organize the Third Ohio Cavalry. He resigned his commission on January 5, 1863.

David S. Stanley was born in Ohio and graduated from West Point in 1852. He fought on the western frontier until the outbreak of the Civil War, when he was assigned to St. Louis, Missouri. Stanley quickly rose to the rank of brigadier and commanded both infantry and cavalry. After participating in the Atlanta Campaign, he was sent back to Tennessee to oppose Hood and won the Medal of Honor at Franklin. He served in the West post-war and ended his career there.

Absent from their troops were almost forty thousand men, who were attempting to protect Rosecrans's and Grant's supply lines. These men would have had much greater value in the upcoming battle along the banks of Stones River.

La Vergne, Tennessee

The Yankees were coming, and Lt. Col. J. D. Webb led the Fifty-First Alabama to meet them. The regiment left their camp on Stewart's Creek near Murfreesboro and moved to La Vergne, Tennessee, about five miles north. Taking a position to the right of the railroad and north of La Vergne, the men dismounted and formed a skirmish line. They did not have long to wait until the U.S. skirmishers leading the advance guard of Rosecrans's army came into view. The advance was led by the Third Kentucky and Seventh Pennsylvania cavalry under Minty.

Infantry and artillery slowly came up on both sides to support the contending cavalrymen, and several probes and counter-probes surged across the fields and through the cedar breaks. Toward the close of the day, the U.S. line grew until it outflanked Wheeler's men on both ends of their line, and their officers ordered a general withdrawal.

Both sides knew what was expected of them, and both followed through on the expectations. The Fifty-First slowly fell back, forcing the advancing U.S. troops to deploy more men. As the day drew to a close, the Confederate cavalry was in the outskirts of the village of La Vergne and the U.S. forces were in line facing them. The weather was cold and damp, and no fires were allowed in the forward positions of either side.[6]

Upton, Kentucky

Early in the morning, Quirk's Scouts reached the Louisville & Nashville Railroad and captured a number of U.S. troops guarding the tracks. Morgan soon came up with the main column, and then the Johnny Rebs experienced one fun moment that they would recall for the rest of their lives. Accompanying Morgan was his favorite telegraph operator, a young man named George Ellsworth, known as "Lightning Ellsworth." Quickly, Ellsworth spliced his key into the line, and soon Morgan was dictating dispatches to U.S. commanders all over Kentucky, sending out false reports of the location and size of the raiding force and asking for details of U.S. troop dispositions.[7]

While Ellsworth was busy tapping out these messages, Morgan sent another regiment to capture the stockade at Bacon Creek Bridge. Thanks to the presence of artillery with the raiders, they quickly achieved this objective and began the main work of the expedition: burning bridges and tearing up rails. Soon, piles of cross-ties were ablaze with iron rails laid over the piles so as to warp and twist the metal.

The Ninth Kentucky passed on to the village of Nolin. The U.S. commander there agreed to surrender if he could be convinced that artillery was in position to fire on him. The Confederate in charge of the negotiations simply took the officer to the gun position, and the Yanks surrendered on the spot.[8]

John Porter of the Ninth Kentucky remembered the day vividly.

> We moved on the direction of Elizabethtown where we knew there was a considerable force of the enemy. We camped about dark at the Red Mills, a few miles from the town and remained unmolested during the night. I well remember how our company looked that night. The night before we were late getting into camp than any of the command, being on the rearguard. On the side of the hill, to the left of the Red Mills, in the edge of a woods, back of a farm which extended down to the pike, we pitched our camp, wet, tired, hungry, and muddy.
>
> Some of us went a half mile for forage for our horses, others set about building fires to warm and cook with. This was a serious undertaking as nothing dry could be found; everything was wet and soggy. By an old log, which I think I at this time would still recognize, we finally got a fire and proceeded to dry and cook. We then lay down on the wet ground and slept soundly until dawn.[9]

New Albany, Mississippi

John K. Mizner resumed his march at dawn on December 26, although without much hope of catching Van Dorn. When the U.S. soldiers reached New Albany, they halted for two hours, time enough for the Seventh Kansas to live up to its established reputation as looters and robbers.

Mizner turned a blind eye to their ransacking while he sent a message to General Grant stating that, in the absence of any large force to the south to block the Confederate column, there was no reason to continue the pursuit. Mizner did continue another six miles before turning back, but he got lost and had to spend the

night in an open bivouac near the Tallahatchie River. It rained
heavily during the night.[5]

Oxford, Mississippi

General Grant finally got some good news. The telegraph was
working again between his headquarters in Oxford, Mississippi,
and Jackson, Tennessee. Now, he could successfully coordinate the
pursuit of Forrest. By this time, Van Dorn was beyond his reach.

Grant sent orders to General Sullivan at Jackson to "make the
best disposition you can to drive Forrest out, and communicate
with me often what you are doing." These dispositions involved
a considerable body of men. Sullivan had 1,000 men at Trenton,
Tennessee; 475 at Humboldt, Tennessee; and 1,000 who were
returning from a futile pursuit of Van Dorn. There were some other
scattered garrisons in addition to the two regiments with Sullivan
in Jackson. Sullivan responded by asking for rolling stock to
transport men by rail and by issuing orders to seize one thousand
horses to mount his infantry.[10]

Nolensville, Tennessee

General Wharton's vedettes fell back along the Nolensville Pike
as Davis and Sheridan's infantry divisions advanced against them.
The blue footsloggers had no cavalry with them, but Wharton
did not have enough men to make a stand against them until he
reached the vicinity of Nolensville. There, Wharton put his brigade
in line and brought up White's Tennessee Battery to support his
deployment. Wharton held this position long enough to force the
Yanks to deploy both men and guns, and, having accomplished his
goal, fell back to Knob Gap, where the roads leading from both
Nolensville and Triune passed through the hills. It was late in the
day, and Wharton hoped that his stand would force his opponent
to bivouac for the night. Instead, Davis's division, the leading U.S.
division, deployed an attack that was delivered with such force
that it drove the Confederate cavalry out of the gap, losing one of
White's guns. With their retreat, quiet fell over the field.[11]

Murfreesboro, Tennessee

Braxton Bragg called a meeting of all of the generals within
reach of his headquarters. As yet, he was not completely sure of
Rosecrans's plans, but it seemed increasingly to be the case that

this was the forward movement for which he had been waiting. In the face of the U.S. move, Bragg needed time to concentrate his infantry. Turning to Wheeler, the commanding general asked how long the cavalry could delay the enemy. Without hesitation, Wheeler replied that he could keep the Yankees away from Murfreesboro for two or three days. Generals Polk and Hardee thought this to be impossible. Bragg issued orders to concentrate the Army of Tennessee at Murfreesboro.[12]

Saturday, December 27, 1862

McKenzie, Tennessee

Forrest led his command into McKenzie during the afternoon. Just six miles ahead was the town of Huntingdon, where the road toward Lexington crossed the Obion River, overflowing its banks with all the recent rain. The crossing point was vital for the escape of the raiders, so Forrest sent Colonel Russell and the Fourth Alabama ahead to secure the bridge. At about 9:00 p.m., a courier arrived back at McKenzie with news that U.S. troops had destroyed all the bridges over the Obion upstream from the Paris-Jackson road. Russell had managed to secure a crossing on the Obion using a neglected bridge in poor repair, but the progress of the main column would be slowed. To gain the time needed to make the crossing, Forrest sent Maj. Nicholas N. Cox with his command to set up a blocking position on the road leading from Paris to Huntingdon.[1]

Grayport, Mississippi

Wet and cold—but jubilant—Confederate cavalrymen followed Van Dorn out of enemy territory across the Yalobusha River at Grayport. They had ridden through Cherry Hill and Pittsborough, but the ride had been without much stress other than the weather, because no Yankees had appeared in pursuit. Now, the men knew themselves to be safe and could concentrate on trying to make themselves comfortable. A sense of accomplishment pervaded the column of tired men as they reflected on what they had done and on what it might mean.[2] Although all of the elements of Van Dorn's command would not reach their assembly area for another two days, the expedition against Holly Springs was effectively over. No cheering citizens greeted the men. The good news had long since been absorbed. Congratulations from headquarters would arrive in due time.

The attitude in Northern circles was quite different. Grant knew that he would have to abandon his attempt to take Jackson and Vicksburg. Sherman was left without support of any kind in making his attack on Walnut Hills.

Walnut Hills, Mississippi

If one stood on high ground, the location was called Walnut Hills, but if one stood on low ground, it was called Chickasaw Bayou. The names may not have been significant, but the perspective was. Defensive positions located on the high ground could be held with smaller numbers, while an attacker on the bottom had to contend with numerous streams and swamps that funneled attacks toward a few crossing points. Sherman used much of the day searching for the best way—or at least an acceptable way—of getting his men into position. On the bluffs, Brig. Gen. Stephen Dill Lee shifted his defenders from point to point and listened with pleasure to the sound of train whistles coming from the direction of Vicksburg. With Grant rendered incapable of forward movement thanks to Van Dorn, reinforcements from the Grenada defense lines were arriving steadily. Lee knew that his defending force would be outnumbered, but the strength of his position on top of the bluffs would make up for a deficiency in numbers—a deficiency that was steadily shrinking.[3]

Crossing of Stewart's Creek, near Murfreesboro, Tennessee

Col. J. D. Webb and the Fifty-First Alabama had been ordered to return to their battlefield of the day before in order to continue their contest with the advance of the Army of the Cumberland. Soon after reaching their previous position, the Fifty-First found itself engaged in battle with a mixed command of U.S. cavalry, infantry, and artillery. To add to the discomfort of being outnumbered and under heavy fire, a drenching rain fell for the rest of the day.

The Fifty-First fell back slowly along the Jefferson Pike, sending out two companies on scouting expeditions toward Buchanan's Mill and La Vergne. Just as the regiment crossed Stewart's Creek, the men came under heavy artillery fire followed by a sharp attack by infantry and cavalry. This skirmish became heavy with losses on both sides. In addition, the Fifty-First had twelve men captured because they were wounded and their horses killed. The regiment had a fireless and ration-less bivouac on the banks of Stones River.[4]

Elizabethtown, Kentucky

Col. H. S. Smith had about 650 men of the Ninety-First Illinois Infantry in Elizabethtown acting as a garrison. Not far from his position were the trestles at Muldraugh Hill, the target of the raid, as the destruction of these works would close the Louisville & Nashville Railroad for a considerable period of time. The Federal Colonel Smith knew a soldier's duty, so he played out his hand to the last. He had his men take position in brick buildings and to prepare loopholes for fighting. He then kept a sharp lookout for Morgan's approach. As soon as Confederate scouts came into view, Smith marched his men around hilltops and between fortified buildings. He hoped to give the impression that he commanded a much larger number of men. His final trick was to send out an officer bearing a flag of truce to hand Morgan a note. The message read:

> To the Commander of the Confederate Forces:
> Sir: I demand an unconditional surrender of all your forces. I have you surrounded and will compel you to surrender. I am, sir, your obedient servant,
> Colonel H. S. Smith

Morgan appreciated the spirit of his opponent, but he did not falter in his approach. Instead, he sent back a message that it was Smith who was surrounded and who needed to surrender. In any case, Morgan had all of the tactical advantages. Smith had his men dispersed in several buildings, and these positions did not offer an interlocking defense. Morgan had a six-to-one advantage in numbers, and, most important of all, he had artillery. Morgan placed his guns in a commanding position on Cemetery Hill and then told Duke to move to the right and Breckinridge to the left and to take the fight to the enemy. Crossing the rain-swollen Valley Creek with their rifles held over their heads, the Confederates braved the freezing water and advanced on the Yankees.

As the Southern fighters moved toward the square, townspeople prudently moved in the opposite direction. When the battle began, both sides put up a hard fight. One of the participants remembered, "John Dunn, a gallant Irishman in our company, made his way to the large brick hotel, full of the enemy, entered it and proceeded to the top of the house. He tore down a Yankee flag that was flying from a pole and, wrapping the flag around his body, made his way down. He came out of the building and crossed to the opposite side of the street, while yet the inmates of the house had not surrendered."[6]

The Confederate artillery had its way, since the U.S. forces had no cannon. Palmer set up his battery on a hill about six hundred yards from the town—out of rifle range but in easy artillery distance—and began to send bricks flying into the Yankee positions. As one strong-point surrendered, Palmer moved his six-pounder guns into the streets of the town and kept on firing. The U.S. infantry did not dare come into the street to fire on the cannon, but, following each discharge, some blue riflemen would dash out in an attempt to shoot down the cannoneers while they loaded fresh ammunition. Soon, a cooperative arrangement arose in which the cavalry held its fire while the artillery fired and then aimed for the bold U.S. troops who exposed themselves in their sights. This kept all blue soldiers under cover.

With rifle-fire whipping through windows and shells crashing through brick walls, resistance was futile. Before he could order his men to surrender, Colonel Smith was wounded by a shell fragment, and all resistance collapsed.[7]

The victorious Confederate soldiers quickly rounded up prisoners and spoils of war. The Raiders now had six hundred rifles and thousands of rounds of ammunition. All of Morgan's men now had good weapons.[8]

Many of the residents of Elizabethtown were pro-Confederate, and they celebrated the discomfit of the Northern troops through offering holiday fare to the Southern boys. John Allan Wyeth recalled that he and his comrades spent the night ensconced in feather beds, the only night during the entire raid when they slept in a bed.[9]

Munfordville, Kentucky

Colonel Harlan had traveled hard to get to Munfordville. He had left Bowling Green by rail after a frustrating trip from Gallatin and had gone only an additional ten miles when another engine broke down, stranding one of his three troop trains. On reaching Munfordville, the Colonel learned that Morgan was well ahead of him and had already captured several U.S. posts. The men under his command were tired out from their two long days on the train, so they were disembarked and marched to the fairgrounds. They had no tents, so the men rested as well as they could on the wet, cold ground. Col. Edward Hobson arrived with some reinforcements: six hundred men, half of them cavalry.[10]

Triune, Tennessee

Gray infantry from Gen. Patrick Cleburne's division arrived to support Wharton's weary cavalrymen. The troops took up a strong defensive position, and the weather turned in the Confederates' favor. A fog blanketed the ground, a fog so heavy that General McCook was afraid to advance his infantry against the Confederate position. The morning slowly passed, and noon came and went with no action on either side. When the fog thinned, the Southern boys abandoned their first line and fell back to another ridge just outside the village of Triune. Skirmishing became almost constant as the U.S. forces probed this new position and brought forth their rifled artillery.

Just as the U.S. artillery had established their superiority and prepared for an infantry assault, it began to sleet. Again, the intervention of the weather allowed the Confederates to fall back yet again, a position that they held until dark.

Even though McCook had not achieved decisive action, he had achieved one important objective. Triune was the crossing of the north-south Nolensville Pike and the east-west Franklin-Murfreesboro Road. By the end of their skirmishes, McCook was in position to move toward the developing Confederate concentration.[11]

Sunday, December 28, 1862

Obion River Bottoms, Tennessee

Forrest knew that two infantry brigades under Sullivan were rapidly approaching his position and that the bridges on the good roads had all been destroyed. There was only one way out of Federal territory: the decrepit bridge Russell had found the night before. As that was all that there was, it would have to make do. However, the bridge was not the only problem. The approach to the structure was a narrow causeway, four hundred yards long, that was water-logged and decaying.

The weather was cold and occasional showers of sleet filled the frigid air, but Forrest and his men waded into the water to become road builders and bridge repairers. Since he commanded so many raw recruits who had just joined his command, Forrest led from the front. He took an axe, found a tree of the proper length, and felled and trimmed the trunk into a pole. This pole he then carried on his shoulder to the bridge and used it to prop up the shaky structure. All through the afternoon and dark night, Forrest worked alongside the crews, making, in the parlance of the time, a full hand.

While one work party shored up the bridge, other men felled and trimmed trees, using the trunks to corduroy the road into a firmer roadbed. When faced with mud holes too deep to be paved with tree trunks, the soldiers reluctantly took sacks of flour and coffee out of the wagons and piled the precious commodities into a make-shift fill so the rest of their supplies could pass.

Among the workers that night were forty-four African Americans who were slaves of Nathan Bedford Forrest. When Forrest had recruited his regiment, he had gone to his plantation and asked for men to volunteer to drive his wagons. He told them that if the South won the war, he would set them free; if the North won, they would be free anyway. Of the forty-four who left with Forrest in 1861, forty-two were present at his surrender at Gainesville, Alabama, in

1865. On this December night, they were indistinguishable from the enlisted men in the Rebel ranks, all laboring to improve the bridge and its approach causeway.[1] Perhaps the men were inspired by Forrest's words that night. The general was not well known for obeying all of the Ten Commandments and outdid himself in a display of creative and comprehensive profanity.

Miller's Farm, near Murfreesboro, Tennessee

Confederate cavalry formed a line across the Nashville Pike near Miller's Farm, some eight miles north of Murfreesboro. Although there was a church nearby, no services were conducted that morning as the Army of the Cumberland was somewhere in the immediate vicinity. The cavalry pickets exchanged an occasional shot with their opposites in blue. Usually, the Sabbath was quiet, but all of this changed when the Third Ohio Cavalry advanced that afternoon. A skirmish resulted in a Confederate retreat and a U.S. pursuit to the banks of Stewart's Creek.

Later in the afternoon, the skirmishing shifted to the banks of Overall Creek on the Wilkinson Pike. The Fifteenth Pennsylvania Cavalry made a successful charge that carried them across the creek. Instead of stopping, the horsemen continued at a gallop down the Pike. They soon found an infantry force of South Carolinians, whose accurate rifle fire emptied a dozen saddles. The Pennsylvania troopers had had enough, and they left the field. Indeed, they played no further role in the campaign.[2]

Walnut Hills, Mississippi

All day long, the U.S. forces had been fighting. Mostly they fought mud, water, and general confusion as to how to get across the numerous bodies of water and confront the Confederates defending Vicksburg. It had been a losing fight, and not much had been accomplished. By the end of the day, Sherman had all four of his divisions on the ground and, more or less, in position. Some stubborn Rebs who held out around Mrs. Lake's plantation seriously delayed their deployment. Now, though, Sherman had decided to proceed with his advantage in manpower.

The Southern defense had increased from a single brigade to four. An additional brigade was in a reserve position near the town racetrack, and an entire infantry division was aboard trains coming from the Grenada front. Not only had Van Dorn's raid on Holly Springs stopped Grant's advance, but also it now permitted strategic movements to reinforce Vicksburg. Sherman's command was about to experience the consequences of Van Dorn's victory.[3]

Muldraugh Hill, Kentucky

This is what Morgan had come for—the trestles that carried the tracks of the Louisville & Nashville across Muldraugh Hill. The hill is actually a range of rugged knobs that begins near West Point, Kentucky, on the Ohio River and runs southeast to the Tennessee state line. In order to keep the Louisville & Nashville track level at the proper grade, engineers had built a series of trestles, each sixty feet in height and nine hundred to more than a thousand feet in length. These wooden structures were vulnerable, and fortifications were in construction when Morgan arrived.

Lt. Col. Courtland Mason commanded two stockades without artillery of approximately seven hundred men of the Seventy-First Indiana and the Seventy-Eighth Illinois. Morgan sent Breckinridge to attack one position and Duke the other. Since Morgan had artillery and Mason had none, the outcome was entirely predictable. To his credit, Mason refused the initial demand to surrender and put up a bold front until Morgan opened with his guns. After a short bombardment, both U.S. positions capitulated, and the series of trestles soon was in flames.

Morgan was glad to have gained the U.S. soldiers' Enfield rifles. Since this was the second time he had captured an Indiana regiment, Morgan had Ellsworth send a telegram to Governor Morton of Indiana suggesting that Morton simply send Morgan the issued weapons and accoutrements and save Morgan the trouble of paroling the men.[4]

For Wyeth, the fighting was more personal:

> When we reached the stockade, from which some of the enemy had escaped, we were ordered to scour the woods for fugitives. About two or three hundred yards from the fort I came upon a stripling, who, hearing some one approaching, bobbed up from behind the trunk of a fallen tree and held up one hand in token of surrender. As no one else was near, I took his gun—a beautiful new Enfield rifle— and accoutrements. He seemed about my age, and I noticed tears running down over his "peach-down" cheeks. His crying quickly aroused my sympathy, and I tried to reassure him by saying, "Don't be afraid; nobody's going to harm you; you'll be paroled right away and can go home." At this he sobbed out "I've got a good mother at home, and if I ever get back I'll never leave her again." By this time my own feelings were getting the better of me, and when he

mentioned his mother the thought of my own so overcame me that I could not keep the tears out of my own eyes as I said to him; "I have a good mother too. Don't you cry anymore." All this occurred as we were walking side by side back to the stockade, my war-spirit no little dampened and the pride of my capture about lost in the sympathy for the captive.[5]

Sgt. Henry L. Stone rode with Morgan, although his home was in Indiana. While at Muldraugh Hill, he wrote to his mother:

At the railroad trestleworks we captured the 71st Indiana, including Billy Brown and Court Mattson. Lt. Col. Brown appered very glad to see me indeed. I was surprised to see him . . . I happened to go up to the house in which Gen. Morgan had his headquarters and I hadn't more than seated myself by the fire when I looked around and recognized Brown sitting by the same fire.

I says, "Hello, Brown, what are you doing here?" He looked for some time and recognized me at last and shook my hand heartily. After talking a little I took my canteen and called him aside to take a heavy horn of good old cognac brandy. I think he took about three drinks. Next morning I wrote a letter and he said he would take it home to you for me, and I think he will.

Mother, to say I've never wished to be at home and sleep once more in a feather bed would be telling an untruth, but I never enjoyed any life as well as this . . . When we'll leave the state I don't know, neither do I know where General Morgan expects to concentrate his forces . . . I's well now excepting a cold. Not a day's sickness nor a dose of medicine have I taken since joining the service . . . I know it'll prove a great benefit to my health and I'll try to prevent it seriously injuring my morals. It is true that I take a little spirits occasionally, for these cold mornings it is beneficial. I've seen almost the infernal regions on earth since I left home but have endured it all and today rejoice that I'm a Confederate soldier . . . I wish I could have been home at Christmas and took some turkey.[6]

It was as well that Morgan had achieved his major objective for the raid. The U.S. command could pinpoint his presence and closed in their pursuit. John M. Porter, Ninth Kentucky, reminisced years later that getting into Kentucky had been easy, but getting out was much harder.[7]

Munfordville, Kentucky

Col. John Harlan led his men out of town at 3:00 a.m. after only a brief rest. He had been joined by the Thirteenth Kentucky Infantry and the Twelfth Kentucky Cavalry, giving him an effective force of twenty-nine hundred men. Harlan took the road for Elizabethtown, but he was more than a day behind Morgan and his men. However, Harlan's men were at a disadvantage in catching up, as his men walked on two legs, as opposed to Morgan's men, who sat on top of horses with four.[8]

Franklin, Tennessee

With Triune about to fall into U.S. hands, it was time for the Confederate cavalry still in Franklin to head out and join the concentration at Murfreesboro. The direct road to Murfreesboro was blocked at Triune, but Col. Baxter Smith led his men southeast from Franklin to Eagleville. From that village, he either could move to Christiana, just south of Murfreesboro, or march via Shelbyville further to the south before turning north to join Bragg. At any rate, at Eagleville, Smith had his men in a good position to scout the next U.S. move and was in no danger of being cut off.

In any case, Baxter Smith would not be on the field for much longer. He would be captured in the spring of 1863 and spend the rest of the war at Johnson's Island Depot of Prisoners of War.[9]

On the Road in West Tennessee

A member of the Thirty-Ninth Iowa (U.S.) recalled the following:

> We have groveled hard all day and still are not more than 20 miles from Trenton owing to a blundering or tratorous guide who had taken us off the road so that our last night march availed us nothing. About noon we stopped, foraging Some beef and we got some flour & sault from the wagons of the other Regiments, about one Quarter Rations. The men, now expecting to return to Trenton, have everything with them trying to carry it on their backs. When one gives out there is no ambulance or wagon for them to get in to rest for a short time so that the suffering has been terrible. The road behind our Regiment is strewn with the blankets and knapsacks abandoned by the men and the men themselves are straggling for miles back. I am likely to have an excellent night of it. The brigade teams have not come up. Col. Dunum [sic] said he would send me word when he would make his head Quarters and when the Train come up I must get Rations for them, but he has forgot to let me know where he keeps himself. Our regiment is in a terrible condition. Nearly one third have not arrived in camp. This can't endure much longer without some change.[1]

Monday, December 29, 1862

Walnut Bluffs, Mississippi

Gen. George Washington Morgan did not want to make the attack, but his commanding officer was adamant. "Here is the route to take," William Sherman said as he pointed to a corduroy bridge across swampy ground straight into the face of the bluffs, where entrenched Confederates waited. Riding away, Sherman sent back a note to Morgan: "Give the signal for the assault. We will lose 5,000 men before we take Vicksburg and we may as well lose them here." By the end of the day Sherman lost 1,776 soldiers.

In contrast, the Confederates lost 187 men. Most of the Confederates in the trenches shooting down Sherman's troops were reinforcements, whose presence was possible only because Van Dorn had forced Grant to retreat.[1] Van Dorn and his men were now safely back in friendly territory, but the effects of their raid would be felt for months to come.

Murfreesboro, Tennessee

The Confederate cavalry performed just as Bragg expected. The horsemen had advanced at daylight, marching until they encountered the advancing U.S. troops. Skirmishing broke out with the cavalry on favorable terrain, waiting for the opposing infantry to deploy and advance. When outnumbered, they fell back to the next favorable position. The time gained was invaluable to Bragg, who waited for reinforcements to his army.

By late afternoon, the cavalry reached the infantry counterpart and reformed to guard the flanks of the battle line. The riders stretched the right flank from Murfreesboro to the Lebanon Pike, a distance of about two miles.[2] Although these men appeared to be settling down for the traditional cavalry role in battle, this appearance was deceiving. These men were about to move against the advancing U.S. forces—as the wartime song said, "go riding a raid."

Wheeler, gathering his cavalry around the Army of Tennessee, commanded four brigades. One brigade, consisting of the First Alabama, the Third Alabama, the Fifty-First Alabama, the Eighth Confederate, Holman's Tennessee Battalion, Douglass's Tennessee Battalion, and Wiggins's Arkansas Battery, was all under Wheeler's command. John A. Wharton commanded the second brigade of the Fourteenth Alabama, the First Confederate, the Third Confederate, the Second Georgia, the Third Georgia, the Second Tennessee, the Fourth Tennessee, Davis's Tennessee Battalion, Murray's Tennessee Regiment, the Eighth Texas, the Twelfth Tennessee Battalion, and White's Tennessee Battery. Wharton's men were poorly armed; most of the soldiers' long weapons were shotguns, and only a minority possessed side-arms. John Pegram led Wheeler's third brigade, which consisted of the First Georgia, the First Louisiana, the First Tennessee, the Sixteenth Tennessee Battalion, and Huwald's Tennessee Battery. A fourth brigade of six hundred men under Abraham Buford was stationed at McMinnville.[3]

John Pegram was a West Point graduate who had served in the Second Dragoons in the West. He had faced Rosecrans at Rich Mountain, where Pegram was forced to surrender. He had then served on the staffs of Bragg and Kirby-Smith before being assigned to a cavalry brigade in November 1862. Abraham Buford of Kentucky had graduated from West Point in 1841 and had served with distinction in the Mexican War. He had resigned from the army and was farming in Kentucky when the Civil War began. He was given command of a small brigade that was recruited in Kentucky during the Perryville Campaign.[4]

As the hours stretched on, fading daylight found the Army of the Cumberland and the Army of Tennessee facing each other just outside of Murfreesboro. Bragg had three brigades of cavalry on hand, as led by Wheeler, Wharton, and Pegram. The first two opposed Rosecrans's advance, but Pegram had been posted on the Lebanon Pike to guard against the approach of U.S forces from the garrison at Gallatin. Bragg must have been unaware that U.S. officers had stripped the Gallatin garrison to minimum strength so that the men could go north to chase Morgan. This lack of intelligence caused Bragg to misposition Pegram. Buford's Fourth Brigade had been at McMinnville, and Bragg ordered this weak unit of just more than six hundred men to the left and rear of Bragg's deployment to take position at Rover, which allowed Bragg to keep an eye on the routes south from Triune and Columbia.

Bragg was pleased with Wheeler and Wharton's performance.

When he wrote his official report in February 1863, Bragg would comment on the skillful manner in which the cavalry was handled. He observed that Wheeler had committed to hold off the U.S. advance for two or three days but actually had delayed them for four. Historian Ed Bearss disagreed with Bragg's analysis, claiming instead that the wet weather and boggy secondary roads slowed Rosecrans's advance much more effectively than the Confederate cavalry.[5]

Flake's Store, Tennessee

Forrest led his snake-like column of Confederate cavalry out of the Obion River Bottoms early in the morning. He personally drove the first wagon across the causeway and over the bridge to demonstrate the stability of the night's work. Twenty men assisted each wagon, and fifty helped the horses pull each cannon. It had been more than a day of strenuous labor for the entire command, but it had been worth it. Only one bolt-hole across the river had been left, and Forrest had led his men through it. Danger still threatened, however, because U.S. troops were closing in rapidly.[6]

Reaching McLemoresville, Forrest paused to feed both men and horses and to rendezvous with Russell and Cox, who had been assigned to guard the crossing. While making this pause, scouts told Forrest that an enemy brigade had passed through McLemoresville not long before he arrived and that General Sullivan was leading his men into Huntingdon.

From Trenton, a road led east to Huntingdon, where it intercepted a north-south road that led from Paris to Huntingdon to Lexington and back to Clifton on the Tennessee River. From Forrest's position at McLemoresville, a country road ran southeast and connected with the Huntingdon-Lexington road. Forrest chose to take this route, avoiding Sullivan's forces at Huntingdon and gaining distance in the race for the river.

Forrest sent Major Cox to Huntingdon to draw the attention of the Yankees and to distract them from Forrest's real position. However, U.S. patrols discovered the location of Forrest's bivouac, and Sullivan ordered men to move forward as soon as it was light enough to see.[7]

When Forrest reached Flake's Store at dark, he was about seven miles from the intersection of the Huntingdon-Lexington Road, also known as Parker's Crossroads.

Rolling Fork River, Bardstown Road, Kentucky

On the morning of December 29, as Morgan began his retrograde move toward Tennessee, he divided his command to achieve a number of objectives: "I sent Colonel L. S. Cluke's regiment with one piece of artillery to attack and burn the bridge over the Rolling Fork; Col. D. W. Chenault's regiment [Eleventh Kentucky Cavalry] and one piece of artillery in advance to burn the stockade and trestle in Boston, and three companies of Breckinridge's regiment and one mountain howitzer to attack at New Haven. Having completed these dispositions I set my command in motion."[8]

David Waller Chenault was a native of Richmond, Kentucky, and a veteran of the Mexican War. A farmer, he was active in local politics when the Civil War began and raised the Eleventh Kentucky Cavalry. He would be killed in action at the Green River Bridge on July 4, 1863, during the Ohio Raid.

Leroy Stuart Cluke was from Montgomery County, Kentucky and also fought in the Mexican War. He was known throughout the South as a horse trader. He was captured during the Ohio Raid and died at Johnson's Island Depot of Prisoners of War.[9]

Not long after Morgan's men moved out on their various assignments, Col. John Harlan's pursuit finally caught up with them. Harlan deployed the Tenth Indiana Infantry, the Fourth Kentucky, the Fourteenth Ohio, and the Seventy-Fourth Indiana along with a battery. When the battery opened fire, the Confederates reacted by beginning a rapid retreat over the rain-swollen Rolling Fork River, leaving a rearguard to make "an obstinate resistance."[10]

Harlan was slow in deploying his men because he was uncertain as to the precise Confederate position, which was concealed in a tree line. He also was sure that Morgan outnumbered him, and he wanted to take as few risks as possible. This deliberation allowed enough time for the men who had been sent to burn the Rolling Fork Bridge to be recalled and successfully rejoin the command. Harlan hesitated when, at a critical point, he saw Confederates move toward a hill on his right and sent most of his men to occupy that position. While the infantry were in motion, Ge. Basil Duke ordered a charge by three companies against a section of Harlan's artillery. This attack forced the gunners to cease fire for about fifteen minutes. During that interval, the Confederates swarmed across the river to safety.[11] The crossing was not without loss—as the last of the men reached the opposite banks, the Union artillery reopened fire. A shell fragment struck Duke in the head, and he fell, unconscious, from his horse. A member of the Ninth Kentucky described the skirmish:

Leaving our encampment we moved on the Bardstown Road and reached Rolling Fork river which, from the recent heavy rains was past fording at the usual crossing. While a party was finding a more shallow ford and leveling the banks to enable the artillery to cross, our rear guard was attacked by a large force of Yankees under Colonel John M. Harlan, who pursued us from Elizabethtown, having come from Louisville by railroad as far as they could, and then on horseback.

This was the most critical position, perhaps, our command ever was in, except possibly when in Indiana and Ohio in 1863. It was absolutely necessary to find a passage cross the angry little stream and how to prevent the Yankees from pressing us was the question. A vigorous charge would have been serious to us.

It was determined to present a bold front and, by sheer boldness, awe them and prevent a charge. General Morgan in person, directed the crossing of the main body of the command while Colonels Duke and Breckinridge with only four companies—ours was one of the four—held at bay the large body of cavalry under General Harlan until the entire command was safe over the river.

The four companies were at the mercy of the Yankees, and they had only to rush on us and destroy or capture us. For some reason they did not charge, though a hot fire was kept on us all the time and their artillery was tremendous. The four companies stretched in a weak line in front of them, bore all this and returned a vigorous and destructive fire. Our horses were a half-mile in our rear on the bank of the river and the shells from the Yankee cannon burst in our company's line, killing five horses outright and knocking half the line down. E. P. Roane, a horse-holder, was seriously wounded.

About the same time a fragment of a shell struck Colonel Duke in the head and he fell senseless from his horse. Colonel Breckinridge, who was at his side, assumed command and directed the movements of the four companies while Colonel Duke was born bleeding from the field across the river. This was a critical moment. All that could be done had been nobly performed. The entire army was now in safety and to our firmness they owed their safety. And now, how were we to be withdrawn to safety?

Finally the four companies gradually began to withdraw, keeping up a constant fire all the time and retreating *backward*. We finally reached our horses only to find many of them killed, wounded and scattered. Fortunately, and for some strange and unaccountable reason, the enemy did not pursue us and we gathered up our wounded, mounted our dismounted men behind us and went safely over the stream.[12]

Duke's wound had a profound effect on the men, as he was a popular officer who had proven his leadership ability on more than one occasion. Capt. Tom Quirk of Quirk's Scouts lifted Duke onto his horse and carried the unconscious officer out of the line of fire. Some of the men under Colonel Harlan, witnessing this event from a distance, were convinced that Duke had been killed. Quirk stopped at the first house that he reached, and his men confiscated a buggy that they then filled with a mattress and bedding. In this make-shift ambulance, Duke, still unconscious, accompanied the column until Bardstown.

On reaching Bardstown, and a temporary degree of safety, Duke was carried into a house, and Dr. Thomas Allen, Second Kentucky, examined the wound. After washing away the clotted blood, was Allen found that a portion of skin and bone behind Duke's right ear had been cut away by an artillery fragment. Just as the doctor finished the examination, Duke opened his eyes and said, "That was a close call!"[13]

Wyeth, a member of Quirk's Scouts, had been in the advance guard once the soldiers crossed Rolling Fork. He remembered that his unit "found shelter in a livery stable and a sound sleep on a corn pile." He also remembered that discipline among the raiders broke down, and they looted a large general store:

> The proprietor had refused to accept Confederate money for his goods, had locked his doors and left town. The men who had crowded in through the doors they had battered down had great difficulty in making their way out with their plunder through a surging crowd that pressed to get in before everything was gone. I was amused at one trooper who induced others to let him out by holding an ax in front of him, cutting edge forward, one arm clasping a bundle of at least a dozen pairs of shoes and other plunder, while on his head was a pyramid of eight or ten soft hats, one on top of the other, just as they had come out of the packing box.[14]

Harlan had had enough. Once Morgan disappeared, the U.S. troops fell back a short distance and went into a defensive position. The hammer in Rosecrans's plan had ceased to swing.

Tuesday, December 30, 1862

Flake's Store, Tennessee

Forrest was aware that two U.S. infantry brigades were in close proximity to his camp, but success only had increased his boldness. Forrest and his men were between the two U.S. forces, so as long as he could keep them separated, he was roughly equal in numbers to each of them. This presented Forrest with the classic military tactic of fighting each enemy unit separately and (hopefully) defeating them "in detail." Either he could continue his retreat or he could stand and fight. Given the possibility of defeating two brigades of Yankees and the attractiveness of an entire day or rest for his men, Forrest halted his movements and held his position at Flake's Store.

Forrest had not chosen the site at random. The store was located at a large spring that provided plenty of water for men and animals, and the owner was pro-Confederate. One of the myths of the Civil War depicts East Tennessee as pro-Union and West Tennessee as rabidly Confederate. The reality was often the reverse, with cities in East Tennessee holding strong Confederate attachments and counties along the north-flowing Tennessee River in the western part of the state expressing a strong streak of Union sentiment. Economics is tied to geography, and the Tennessee River gave some West Tennessee counties a strong relationship with St. Louis and Louisville. The politics of these counties, not surprisingly, followed the money. Thus, Forrest was operating in an area where many civilians were quite willing to pass on information about his movements to U.S. forces. Mr. Dudley Flake, the store owner, had a son in the Confederate Army.[1]

Forrest did not allow all his men to remain idle. He sent Col. James Starnes with his regiment toward Huntingdon to keep an eye on the U.S. forces there. One of the men in Starnes's unit, Dan Beard, wrote:

We halted at noon at a crossroads leading from Huntingdon to McLemoresville. After feeding the horses the men dropped down wherever they could and were soon fast asleep. I hitched to a bush close beside the road, kicked the snow off a brush pile, and went to sleep on it with my shotgun in my arms. I don't know whether I slept a minute or an hour, but I awoke amid a most infernal din of firearms, clattering of horses feet and yells. It was a minute or two before I could realize where I was and what it all meant. I saw a detachment of Federal cavalry, about eighty in number, pass me in a sweeping gallop with drawn pistols, coming from the direction of Huntingdon. Just past me some Confederates had formed and poured a volley into them which sent them flying past me, and I fired both barrels at them from a distance of less than twenty feet with no visible effect. I loaded and capped my gun with fingers so numb I could not feel the caps, mounted, and set off in a gallop after the fleeing Yankees. On the road we found one dead Yankee and two of our men coming back wounded.[2]

Forrest was duly informed of the skirmish, but it did not alter his plans. Beard's account, however, does note two important points. First, Forrest had not trained his men to the level of discipline needed to be fully effective, else an eighty-man patrol would not have stumbled on a sleeping regiment. Second, despite his success in capturing men and weapons, some of the Confederates were still armed with inferior guns.

Forrest also sent Colonel Biffle with his regiment back toward Trenton to deal with an isolated force of U.S. soldiers who foolishly had returned to the area with only 120 men. These troops found themselves prisoners of war before the close of the day. With that accomplished, Biffle returned to Forrest.[3]

Following the skirmish between the U.S. cavalry patrol and Starnes's regiment, U.S. Col. Cyrus Dunham led his fifteen-hundred-man brigade out of Huntingdon at about noon and marched towards Clarksburg, south of Huntingdon and in the direction of Parker's Crossroads.

Dunham was from Courtland, Indiana, and had served two terms in the U.S. Congress. He was in command at Munfordville, Kentucky, when Bragg moved north in the fall of 1862, and allowed his command to be trapped with no choice but to surrender. He was looking for a way to redeem his reputation as a soldier.

About the time that Dunham left Huntingdon, Capt. William Forrest (Nathan Bedford Forrest's younger brother) led his company of scouts east from Forrest's position at Flake's Store to picket the road to Parker's Crossroads. He took position at Clarksburg. When

U.S. infantry began to arrive in the darkness, a skirmish broke out, and Capt. Forrest took enough prisoners to determine that a major force—Dunham's—had reached the village. The presence of the Confederates told Dunham that his opponent probably would head for Parker's Crossroads early the next morning.[4]

Lt. Ayers recorded his experiences in his journal. "The 50th Indiana were ordered out and had a little fight. They routed a lot of Rebels who were camped out of town a piece nicely. We were within a short distance of them but we lay and slept and knew nothing of it until the morning. We did not start very early nor have we marched very far."[5]

Jefferson, Tennessee

Late in the afternoon of the previous day, Wheeler had received orders to lead his fatigued soldiers on a raid against Rosecrans's supply line. He had assembled his men in a cold rain and led them north along the Lebanon Pike during the small hours of December 30. The command reached a point some miles east of Jefferson when they received news that the village was occupied by Starkweather's brigade of U.S. infantry. With the assistance of local men who knew the byways, Wheeler circumvented Jefferson and blocked the northern pike. When the first wagons of a sixty-four-wagon train pulled into Starkweather's camp to move toward Jefferson, Wheeler struck.

Wheeler sent one detachment to hit the wagons that were still on the road, while the rest of the command dismounted and formed a line for an attack on the surprised U.S. infantry. The Twenty-First Wisconsin Infantry was the first ready to move, and they were sent to the rescue of the wagons still on the road. Wheeler's men were not to be denied, however, and the infantry fell back to a log farmhouse on a hill and made a defensive stand. Starkweather then sent a patrol of about fifty men to outflank the gray cavalry and relieve the wagon train. The Confederates discovered this patrol and beat it back. By this time, the rest of the Union brigade was in formation and marched to the hill occupied by the Twenty-First Wisconsin. Wheeler had no intention of attacking uphill against fully formed infantry, so he rounded up his men and left the field, leaving behind twenty burning wagons and taking with him fifty prisoners. In order to protect the supply route, U.S. officials ordered Starkweather to hold his infantry at Jefferson instead of moving on to Murfreesboro. Already, Wheeler's strike had a strategic as well as a tactical effect on the developing battle. Starkweather's brigade would not be usable until January 1.[6]

John C. Starkweather was from Cooperstown, New York. He was living in Milwaukee in 1861 when he was given command of the First Wisconsin Infantry. He rose to brigade command and fought at Perryville, Stones River, Chickamauga, and Chattanooga. Placed in command at Pulaski, Tennessee, in 1864, he was defeated by Nathan Bedford Forrest. Starkweather resigned from the army in 1865 and returned to Milwaukee, where he died in 1890.

On the Road to Springfield, Kentucky

Spirits were high in Morgan's command. They had achieved the main objective of their raid with light casualties and weak opposition. Now, the men were on the road back to Tennessee, and, while they knew that danger and difficulties were ahead of them, they had great confidence in themselves and in their leader. Wyeth recalled that the men sang and joked as they began their long day's ride. One of the favorite songs that ran up and down the column was "Lorena." The song's lyrics, "The snow is on the grass again," soon proved to be true. At about noon, clouds gathered, and a cold rain, which soon turned to sleet, began to fall.

When the men reached Springfield, Morgan allowed the men a brief rest, but he knew that a large U.S. force was in Lebanon, only a few miles away. He needed to be beyond their grasp by morning. While most of the men rested, Morgan sent Cluke's Scouts to the outskirts of Lebanon with orders to drive in the outposts and build a long line of fires to make it appear that Morgan's whole force was present and preparing to attack in the morning. Wyeth, one of the Scouts, wrote that he and his comrades piled rails and built fires until late in the night.

At Springfield, Morgan called his men back into formation and, as the scouts built fires, the main column passed around Lebanon for Campbellsville and safety. None of the men who made that night march ever forgot it. The road was obscure, the artillery frequently had to be helped out of the mud, and sleet fell the whole time. When the sky finally became light the next morning, a coat of ice and icicles plastered every man's beard and every horse's mane.[7]

La Vergne, Tennessee

Wheeler led his men west toward the Murfreesboro-Nashville Pike in keeping with his orders to disturb Rosecrans's communications. Along the way, the soldiers caught and paroled two small parties of Yanks. Wheeler learned from his advance scouts that La Vergne was full of blue coats and that wagons choked the surrounding fields. Wheeler decided to make a three-pronged attack from the southeast, north, and northwest. It took only a brief fusillade of pistol fire to convince the surprised wagoners and their guard to throw down their weapons. Quickly, Wheeler and his men tallied seven hundred prisoners, released them to make their way back north, and set three hundred wagons on fire.[8]

Wheeler did not linger to enjoy his victory, because scouts told him that another U.S. brigade was approaching. Gen. Moses Walker led the Seventeenth, the Thirty-First, and the Thirty-Eighth Ohio Infantries and the Fourth Michigan Artillery. He had left one regiment, the Eighty-Second Indiana, to guard his camp. From a hill some six hundred yards outside of La Vergne, Walker saw Wheeler's sea of destruction. A few Confederates were still attempting to corral the mules that had pulled the wagons, so Moses ordered his artillery to open fire, but all this accomplished was to scatter the mules. The Rebs soon left the scene. Walker decided to remain at La Vergne in order to guard the route to Nashville, thus depriving Rosecrans of yet more men.

Walker was an attorney from Fairfield County, Ohio, and a graduate of Yale. He became colonel of the Thirty-First Ohio when the war began and served at Perryville and Stones River. Badly wounded at Chickamauga, he was out of action for the rest of the war.

Pressing on to Rock Springs, the men following Wheeler disbanded another small wagon train and then fell like lightning from the clouds on Nolensville, where no one expected them. The weary but elated men paused for the night some five miles from Nolensville.[9]

Capt. George K. Miller of the Eighth Confederate Cavalry rode with Wheeler. When time allowed, a few days later, he wrote home:

> We were roused from our slumbers at midnight, saddled up, mounted and in a few minutes were following General Wheeler up the Lebanon road. It was raining and so dark that one could not see the troopers by his side. When we struck the ford at Stones River we only knew we were riding in water by the splashing noise of our horses' feet. Proceeding out of camp about five miles and crossing to the north side of the river we continued about two miles, then left the Lebanon Pike and took the one leading to the little village of Jefferson, directly in the rear of the Yankee army. Daylight found us near that village, where we halted and fed our horses. Soon in the saddle again, leaving the main road, we took by paths and about noon came up close to the village of La Vergne. Into this we dashed—four

or five regiments of us—at full speed, firing a few shots as we rode. At once we found in our possession a large train, over 300 heavily loaded wagons with quartermaster and commissary stores, and some 300 prisoners captured. The officers went quickly to work paroling the prisoners while the men burnt the wagons. It was a sight to make rebeldom glad. Mules, stampeding with burning wagons hung in their traces. Yankees running, all appliances for our subjugation!

Applying the spurs for two hours we dropped like a tornado on quiet little Nolensville. Here is La Vergne repeated. We found squads of Yankees here and there and some 150 wagons, mostly loaded with ammunition and medicines, together with several fine ambulances. These latter we preserved; the other we set the flames upon. The Yankees we sent on their way rejoicing, as paroled prisoners of war, back to their New England households.

We tarried but a short time at N., then pushed down into a little valley where we found large numbers of their wagons filled with corn, bedclothing, poultry, house-furniture, eggs, butter, etc. of which they had just plundered farms. We relieved them of their plunder, put the prisoners bareback on mules, burned the wagons, and rode on.

Four hundred and fifty to five hundred wagons, 600 prisoners, hundreds of mules and horses captured, and we had an immense deal of fun.[10]

There is no doubt that the Confederates did have a great deal of fun. They ran amok along the U.S. supply lines and had the pleasure of ransacking numerous sutler wagons as well as destroying military supplies. There can be no accurate count of the wagons destroyed, however, because the numbers reported from all sources vary so greatly. Included in the number are baggage wagons for officers, sutler wagons, and vehicles loaded with military equipment.

Murfreesboro, Tennessee

As the cold, soggy day faded into darkness, the men of both armies settled down for what rest they might be able to get. As they did so, somewhere in the gathering gloom, a band began to play. Soon other bands tuned up. "Yankee Doodle" was answered by "Dixie," "Hail, Columbia" dueled with "The Bonnie Blue Flag." It is agreed that a U.S. band first raised the tune "Home, Sweet Home," but soon all the bands took up the refrain. When the last note was played, stillness covered the field.[11]

Wednesday, December 31, 1862

Clarksburg, Tennessee

The U.S. bivouac was astir before dawn. Colonel Dunham, like any good officer, fed his men before putting them on the march for Parker's Crossroads. When he reached it, Dunham expected Forrest to be to the northwest, coming from the direction of McLemoresville and Flake's Store. This placed Dunham between Forrest and the crossing point of the Tennessee River.

Dunham reached the strategic crossroads and cleared it of the Confederate pickets he expected to find there. Posting one regiment at Parker's Crossroads and another on the road back to Clarksburg, Dunham sent the Fiftieth Indiana, part of the Eighteenth Wisconsin, and three guns of the Seventh Wisconsin Artillery up the McLemoresville Road to look for Forrest. They found him.[1]

Parker's Crossroads was so named because it was the residence of the Reverend John Parker and his wife, Rebecca. Parker was seventy-eight years old and had provided spiritual guidance to the people of the area for more than a generation. He had opposed secession and proudly supported the Union—until the war landed in his front yard and Union troops placed cannon in his door. When Reverend Parker died in 1864, he gave instructions that instead of a traditional east-facing grave, he wanted to be interred facing north, so that on Resurrection morning he could "Kick the Yankees back where they belong."

McLemoresville Road, near Parker's Crossroads, Tennessee

Before breaking camp, Forrest called Maj. W. S. McLemore of the Fourth Tennessee Cavalry to his side. Forrest knew from his scouts that more Yanks were at Huntingdon, north of Clarksburg.

With Dunham far ahead of his friends, Forrest intended to attack and defeat the exposed brigade before help could arrive. He needed to know what the relief column of Yanks was doing and to delay their march as much as he could. Forrest gave both verbal and written orders to McLemore to move to Clarksburg. He intended for McLemore's battalion to join Capt. William Forrest's Scouts, delay the U.S. advance, and keep him fully informed of the progress of the Yankees near Parker's Crossroads. However, the verbal and written orders did not correspond—some things were unclear, and McLemore was uncertain as to his duty as events unfolded.

The written orders that McLemore received led him to believe that he was to make a reconnaissance at Clarksburg, where he would meet Capt. William Forrest. Once he completed the reconnaissance, the Major thought that his orders were to return immediately to the main body.[2] However, this was not necessarily what Forrest had intended.

Moving toward Parker's Crossroads, the main body of Confederates reached a large field belonging to a farmer named Hicks. Spotting the Wisconsin and Indiana troops on the far side of the field, Forrest deployed the Fourth Alabama and the Eighth Tennessee. Forrest personally chose Sgt. Nat Baxter, a member of Morton's Battery, to take his howitzer to within four hundred yards of the U.S. line and to open fire on the Seventh Wisconsin Artillery. This was the first—but not the last—time that Forrest used his artillery at unconventionally close ranges to defend or attack a position or. Baxter described the situation:

> Very early on the morning of December 31st General Forrest rode up to our battery and ordered me to hitch up my gun and come with him. Having gone about a half-mile in the direction of Parkers Cross Roads he ordered some cavalry that accompanied him to throw the fence down and here we turned into a field with the piece. General Forrest dismounted and went ahead to the crest of a hill and selected a position for my gun. To my great surprise, as I reached the top of the hill, I saw the Federals in heavy line of battle not more than four hundred yards away. With the exception of two or three hundred cavalry immediately behind my gun, and one or two hundred dismounted men, who were about one hundred yards in front, behind logs and in fence corners skirmishing with the enemy, there were no other Confederate soldiers in sight. He told me to open immediately on them, which I had no sooner done that three pieces of artillery from the Union side responded in lively fashion. I succeeded in dismounting one of the guns to the great satisfaction of General Forrest, who remained with me

all through the duel, and was with my piece at frequent intervals throughout the day.[3]

The U.S. infantry made more than one foray across Hicks's field, but always they were forced back by the fire of the dismounted troopers and by copious amounts of cannister from Baxter's gun. Commenting on this fight, Private Baird said: "We did not much fear to charge a line of Yankee infantry who fired by volley or command. It looked to be probably that every one of our men would be killed or wounded, but these terrible volleys were often without effect, as the Confederate lines were open, and all the men who could were behind some obstacle, and when they could deliver their fire it was effective."[4]

At about 9:00 a.m., seeing no advantage to be gained by staying where he was, Dunham fell back and united his troops some twelve hundred yards southeast of Parker's Crossroads. The U.S. position ran along a ridge with the wagon train sheltered in a hollow on the reverse slope.[5]

This new position left the road to Lexington (and subsequently the Tennessee River) open, and Forrest took advantage of this to begin sending his wagons on toward safety. Dunham was not going to let Forrest slip away, so he ordered his men forward to a position along a fence closer to the Parker dwelling and parallel to the road Forrest was using. This latest U.S. line had its left on the Huntingdon-Lexington Road and its right anchored in an open field. From left to right, Dunham commanded one company of the 50th Indiana, the 39th Iowa, the 122nd Illinois, a detachment of the 18th Illinois Mounted Infantry, and the rest of the 50th Indiana. The guns of the 7th Wisconsin Battery were nestled between the 39th Iowa and the 122nd Illinois.

Forrest continued moving into Parker's Crossroads, and his numbers seemed huge to the waiting Yankees. The colonel of the 122nd Illinois, John L. Rinaker, thought that Forrest had about six thousand men, with two thousand of them forming for the attack at any given time.[6] This was the 122nd's first experience in combat.

Because of the direction of the Confederate advance, Dunham again adjusted his line, moving north eight hundred yards and forming an east-west line facing north. The Southern soldiers took up a position that paralleled the Union position. Less than six hundred yards separated the opposing lines. Forrest once again sent his artillery on the offensive, running his guns forward to within three hundred yards of the U.S. infantry. Soon, the artillery dominated the field, and the 50th Illinois and 122nd Illinois's attempt to crack the Rebel line was shot to pieces long before the charge could drive home. Lt. A. L. Huggins described the fight from the Southern perspective: "When charged upon, Baxter would pour grape and canister into the advancing line, which suddenly and effectually checked the charge. The enemy were so close to us that Dibrell's men (supporting the battery) were compelled to load and fire lying down. At this crisis Lieut. Baxter did the loading of his gun of our battery himself, lying upon his back and ramming home the charge."[7] Baxter's gun was a mountain howitzer, so it was quite possible for the gunner to load and fire it from a prone position.

From the Union side, Pvt. W. H. Peter, 122nd Illinois, wrote: "At half past 11 we were brought under a terrific fire of shell, grape, and canister. We lay behind a fence at the edge of a strip of timber while across in front of us some 500 yards wee planted the enemy cannon they were planted on a ridge and were in full view and had we not lain down where we were there many more must have been killed."[8]

Dunham's situation was becoming more desperate each minute. An unsuccessful attack on his left by Confederates led by Alonzo Napier, who was killed in the assault, was only the prelude to a Confederate movement that enveloped both his flanks. Starnes's regiment returned from its detached duty and was sent around the Union left. Russell's Alabama regiment and Woodward's Kentucky troopers withdrew from the main battle line to turn the right. At the same moment, Confederate artillery surged forward, which unlimbered at ranges as short as two hundred yards from the Union-held rail fence. The U.S. line began to crumble under this attack. The colonel of the Thirty-Ninth Iowa, H. J. B. Cummings, described the scene. He was attempting to rally his men, when they

> . . . mistook the command for an order to retreat and commenced breaking to the rear from near the right of the regiment, which, despite my efforts, became propagated along the entire line. I hastened toward the right of the retreating men and ordered a halt and the command to form, and had done much toward reforming when we were opened upon by a heavy fire of dismounted men who had advanced under cover of the thick underbrush to within 50 feet of my men. They then in more confusion fell back toward a fence, and received standing the fire of the enemy's artillery and under it and the fire from the rear the confusion became worse.
>
> Under the fire, so unexpected from both front and rear . . . about half of my regiment broke to the left of our line as formed behind the fence and crossed the [Lexington] road into the cornfield upon the opposite side.

Assisted by a number of senior officers I attempted to halt and reform the scattered men, the enemy turned their canon upon us and we were fired upon by their cavalry, and I was unable to form a line until we reached a skirt of timber about a quarter of a mile from where we had laid in line.[9]

Dunham's command was now split into two main groups and many small fragments. One group was still in the general vicinity of the east-west line marked by a rail fence, and another group, which included Dunham, had been driven toward Lexington several hundred yards to the vicinity of a community called Red Mound. The wagon train had been unable to evacuate its position and had been captured. Confederate Sgt. John Strange took taking inventory of the contents of the wagons.

Nat Baxter remembered that "white flags appeared all along the Union line. I was under the impression that they had surrendered, and had gone in front of my gun toward the Federal line to converse with one of their officers. Just at this moment a roll of small arms was heard immediately behind the location of our batteries and in our rear. I rushed back to my gun to see what had happened and about this moment General Forrest came up to me, ordering me to limber up my piece and leave the field, pointing in the direction we were to go."[10]

Dunham was unaware that part of his command was attempting to surrender. Forrest, who was in the concentration of Confederates confronting Dunham, sent in a flag of truce of demanding a surrender. Dunham briskly rebuffed it, but Forrest returned the flag a few minutes later with a second demand. Dunham refused to discuss a cease-fire, and the messenger returned to Forrest.

On the Huntingdon Road, to Parker's Crossroads via Clarksburg

U.S. Col. John W. Fuller had his men on the road from Huntingdon at 5:30 a.m. They reached Clarksburg at about 10:30 a.m. and were joined by General Sullivan, the commander of U.S. forces at Jackson. Sullivan, with his mounted escort, rode out of Clarksburg while Fuller allowed his men a rest. The general had not ridden far when a Confederate patrol fired on him. This was the rearguard of Maj. W. S. McLemore's force.

Fuller was not shaken by the sound of firing. The England native had been in Ohio when the war began and had raised a regiment for the Union. He and his men had seen service at Iuka and at Corinth, where he won a commendation for his coolness under fire.

McLemore had been puzzled by the absence of William Forrest's Scouts. He would learn later that the company had fallen back early that morning when Dunham had advanced from Clarksburg. Soon, McLemore could hear the sound of the guns at Parker's Crossroads, but he knew that he was in the rear of Dunham's forces, which had moved in that direction. Instead of marching down the main road, the major decided to move east and south by country lanes. Only his rearguard remained and, following their clash with Sullivan, they too went south.

McLemore and his men would not reach the battlefield at all that day. When the sounds of battle ceased, McLemore wisely led his men due east and crossed the Tennessee a couple of days later. He rejoined his regiment near Columbia, Tennessee, in mid-January. This misadventure, arising from unclear orders, left Fuller's U.S. brigade a clear and unopposed line of march into the rear of Forrest's position.[11]

Fuller reached a hill crest north of Parker's Crossroads and, from his position, he had a full view of the field. General Sullivan quickly approved an attack, so Fuller deployed the Twenty-Seventh and Sixty-Third Ohio on the left of the Huntingdon-Lexington road and the Thirty-Ninth Ohio on the right. The Seventh Wisconsin Artillery unlimbered to the left of the road also. This formation surged into the rear of Forrest's main artillery position and caught the horse holders of Dibrell's and Cox's commands by surprise, stampeding the horses and capturing three hundred men. The Seventh Wisconsin sprayed shell into the fugitives who broke away from Fuller's charge.[12]

Instead of defeating his enemy in detail, Forrest found himself trapped between the two forces.

Red Mound, Tennessee

Forrest sat on his horse awaiting Dunham's reply to Forrest's demand for surrender when Col. Charles Carroll dashed up with the news that "a heavy line of infantry is in our rear." Carroll finished with the cry, "What will we do?"[13] It may be that Forrest had little use for Carroll, a man who had been assigned to Forrest as inspector general. Carroll had been in command of the Fifteenth Tennessee Infantry but had lost control of his men while on a march and had gotten into a public shouting match with his subordinate officers. Court-martialed and assigned to staff duty, Carroll would be captured in February 1863. He did not return to duty for the rest of the war.[14] Whatever his inner reaction, on the exterior, Forrest was calm. Tradition claims that Forrest replied, "Do? We'll charge 'em both ways!" In effect, that is what happened.

Starnes and Russell stepped up their attack on Dunham to prevent him acting in concert with Fuller. Forrest ordered his Escort Company, a detachment of the Eighth Tennessee, and everyone else he could round up, to join him in a gallop to the east of the Reverend Parker's house. Once in a favorable position, the men formed a line and charged Fuller's flank. The attack was a success.

Nat Baxter was following his gun off the field, attempting to escape toward Lexington, when Forrest personally ordered Baxter to join the line forming for the charge. Baxter protested that, as an artilleryman, he had no sidearms and was entirely without weapons. Forrest told him to get in line anyway, as he noted, "I want to make as big a show as I can." Baxter charged the Union line empty-handed.[15]

Forrest's Escort had been recruited in the summer of 1862 and had joined him at La Vergne, Tennessee, in September. The West Tennessee Raid was their first major experience in combat, but they had already proven themselves as a force to reckon with. As the war progressed, Forrest would use this company-sized unit as a shock force. Parker's Crossroads was the first time he did so. Among the members of the Escort who made the attack with Forrest was Johnston Ryall. He wrote home after the battle:

> Lying on my back I will endeavor to let you know that I am in good spirits and health save a broken leg. I feel pretty low this morning since I have had my leg splinted. I spent rather a bad time from yesterday two o'clock in the morning, lying on the floor of a negro cabin with little cover on me, no fire scarcely, and helpless. I can't say the Yankees are kind to the helpless. I had dismounted with John Bryant, a messmate who was wounded in the shoulder, on the field and the captain commanding told me to get on my horse and leave him which I did, and on reaching the company which was still under fire Ton Story's mare kicking with great force struck me on the left leg, four inches below the knee and shivered the shin bone. The doctor who dressed it this morning says he thinks it will get well before a great while. I was fearful from the pain that I would have to lose it, now with care I hope not. I tried to stay on my mare when kicked, but she was unmanageable and having no use of one

leg I could not stick on so I tumbled off and scrambled in a fence corner (I was in a lane) and there had to lie until picked up. I shall try to be conveyed to a Mr. Fearson's house some two miles from here towards Lexington and remain there till I get able to travel and then I can work my way home, be exchanged if able, if not perhaps can assist on the farm. You need not be uneasy. I think I shall not want for anything to make me comfortable. I hope in some five or six weeks that I may move about. I much regret that after the fight was so near over I should have been kicked by a horse. I wish the leaders in this war could feel the suffering around me. There are many much worse wounded than I.[16]

In response to the bold attack by a handful of Confederate cavalry, General Sullivan ordered Fuller's men to take up defensive positions around the Reverend Parker's house, thus opening the door to a road leading to Lexington. Forrest's command lost no time in seizing the opportunity to leave. Starnes and Russell were the last off the field, as they kept pressure on Dunham to prevent an immediate pursuit. The confusion caused by the attack also allowed the recapture of some of Dibrell and Cox's horses and the release of some of the horse holders. Forrest did lose 3 guns, 8 limbers, 5 wagons, 100 killed or wounded, and 250 captured. U.S. losses from all causes were about 250 men.[17]

Among the wounded Forrest was forced to leave behind was J. M. Metcalf of Lincoln County, Tennessee, who had joined Freeman's Artillery just prior to the expedition. Although he was nineteen years old, Metcalf was of so slight a build that he looked sixteen. He had found the first days of the raid exhilarating, filled with rapid movement, just enough fighting to be exciting, and constant victories that allowed him to equip himself in a proper military fashion, even though when he got a pair of cavalry boots from the stores captured at Trenton, he found one boot to be larger than the other. His luck changed at Parker's Crossroads, where he served as driver on a swing horse in a gun team. His gun was changing position when Fuller's force came up in Forrest's rear and so was in good shape to leave the field. Forrest, however, included the gun in his charge on the U.S. lines, and, in the attack, the driver of the lead and wheel horses were shot off their mounts. Unable to steer the gun from his position on the swing horse, Metcalf found himself being drawn at full speed parallel to the U.S. line with, it seemed, every man shooting at him personally. When the gun struck a log, Metcalf was thrown from his horse and was run over by the wheel horse, the limber chest, and the gun itself. He was captured and taken to a hospital but received no care for several days. When he did receive treatment, doctors found that he had several broken ribs and a broken collarbone. Combined with internal injuries, Metcalf was unfit for duty and was paroled.[18]

As darkness fell, the U.S. troops bivouacked on the field at Parker's Crossroads, and Forrest's men camped in Lexington. In the U.S. camp, Lt. Ayers wrote a long description in his journal of the battle as he had experienced it:

> This has been a great day for our Regiment and our Brigade. We left camp very early this morning. I was ordered to forage for two waggons and teams for ambulances which I did early in the morning and when I joined the Brigade they were drawn up in line of battle at a small place called by some Parkers Cross road and two of our pieces of Artillery were over in an open field sending shell into an ajoining wood with but little effect. One, however, was directed at and went through an old house just in the edge of the wood, made about as great a scattering of Secesh as has been seen lately. It proved from the appearance to be a lot of Secesh Officers taking breakfast which or shells slitely disturbed. We found a fine breakfast in there all pre paired.
>
> While in this position our Co. was detailed to guard the waggon train. This suited me as in the case there should be a battle Col. Cummings had given me permission to join them. They were assisted in this by one Company of the 122nd Reg Illinois Vol, the Rebels appeared to be on the West of the road on which we had taken position. Two Companies of the 59th Indiana were thrown forward as Skirmishers and soon the whole command followed down the Cross Road towards the enemy. I did not accompany them but had to remain at our old position with the Train.
>
> After they had been gone about a half hour we heard some considerable canonading and a little musketry. Col. Cummings' orderly came to me and said "the Colonel" ordered the train to move on down the road. We at once moved it out and had just got nicely at the corners of the Cross roads, in the way, when Col. Dunnum came up and ordered the train to halt, ask who the hell ordered it out and reprimanded the Brigade Quartermaster severely for moving without orders. We remained there a full half hour and the Brigade coming back on the retreat were mixed up with us in a pretty fix. I wonder that the Enemy had not come down on us then. If they had made a charge while we were there and they had ample time, the consequences must have been serious. I trembled all the time we were there freely.
>
> Col. Dunnum, having reconnoitered both Roads, came back and ordered us on and the brigade also moved on and took position

about a half mile down the North and South Road. The Brigade Quartermaster ordered the train in a position in the road of a hollow some 200 yards in the rear of the troops. It was in a bad position and very difficult to get out of. I protested against tasking the few teams of our Reg. into such a hole as they were very heavily loaded. It would be almost impossible for me to get out, but he swore that he commanded that train. He was considerably knettled because of the rebramand he had received from the Colonel.

There was three Quartermasters with the train, those of each Regiment. One of the others and myself left the train, riding up to where one Battery was positioned. From here we could plainly see the Enemy filing down the Road and out of the wood. It was not more that half or three quarters of a mile off and there is no denying they made an imposing appearance. There was asertained to be 8000 Cavalry and mounted Infantry and two Batteries with 8 pieces. They covered over an emence tract of country. Their was between them and us only an open field, a large Cotton field. Their guns and sabers glemed in the sun and they evoked like an enormous host to move against our little force of about 1600. I should just then like to have seen the other Brigade of our expidition coming up about that time. While there I saw one of our shells burst in the Road square among the Rebels. It made a large clear place and to night I hear it killed Col. Napier and four men. All events, a Secesh Colonel is laying near there dead. He is a fine looking man. Our other shells went very wide of the mark. In fact, most of the Artillerymen are drunk and the one who trained the gun for the shell that I spoke of above is he only one that was sober.

I had just returned to the train when along came Col. Dunnum and curdsed the Brigade QM in the most awful manner and ordered him to join his company and for the ranking QM to take charge of the Train. As the #3 QM was still away, the train was in my charge and I proceeded at once to get it out of there and had just got settled in what appeared to me a good place when the Rebel's shells began to drop among the teams thick and fast. These were the first shells I had heard and I must say I thought they made the most frightful screaming imaginable and I guest the Guard (who of course had followed us around) thought about the same thing for they fell on the ground and squated in a manor that would have been ludicrous at another time. But worse was the Negro drivers and some of the white ones who were leaving about as fast as their limbs would carry them on.

The Train had to be got out of that at once. At a hint from one of the Commissary Sergeants, we all took out after the traiterous Negroes and drivers and by a exebition of our Revolvers we soon had them back and as they were were a large number of extray Colored

Persons along, fences were thrown down and we were soon moving. While there, a fuse shell burst immediately over my head sending the shot and pieces on every side of me and striking my Horse in two places. Had the fuse of that shell been a little longer it wound have been a bad piece of work for me. I shall always be greatful to the fellow that cut off that fuse. I directed the train over behind a little wooded knowl where it was comparatively safe. On the other QM coming back I was relieved from my command not a little to my gratification.

We were just congratulating ourselves on getting where we were safe from the Rebel shells when we discovered a large force of the enemy moving in our rear. They were coming up in a line preparatory to a charge. There was two Regiments of them. Some prisoner told me to night there were 1100 hundred of them. I concluded it was about my time to go with my company which I did. They were drawn up with the other company of the guard on a little knowl in the open field where the enemy had the best kind of chance to ride through them.

Both Companies were commanded by 2nd Lieuts. and it was doubtful which ranked the other. Rawls was for deploying out across the Road. The other wanted to do something else. Rawls commenced to execute his plan when a Sert. from some Reg., I don't know where thought Rawls was going to run and raised his gun to him. Rawls was now on the fence and there was no little confusion. Colonel Dunnum's Adjunt came about that time for the ammunition wagons and told them to fire from where they were. I reached them about that time having let my horse slide. After firing two rounds they retired about 50 yards to a house and some Negro quarters situated on a little knowl, well fenced in. While retiring to this position, it was as question with me if the command could be allied at that point but when it arrived my fears were quickly dispelled by seeing the men turn into the yard and fall in line if not in excellent order with the exception of few men of the 122nd Illinois Reg. who passed directly on to their regiment.

In the mean time the Rebels charged up and as the last of our men came into the yard their balls rattled against the fence and whistled about our ears. Our men immediately fired a volley and reloaded. In fact, our men loaded and fired with astounding rapidity. The enemy was soon thrown into confusion and retreated. While they were near their bullets rattled against the quarters of the Negroes like hail and they must have punished us severely ha they not fired so high. As it was, they did us but little damage. They soon rallied and came upon us again. They came in better order this time and the earth shook under their horse tread. Our little band stood their ground and poured the led into them with astonishing activity and again they broke and run without doing us much damage. But this time some of them dismounted and getting behind stumps and whatever would cover them, and acted as Sharp Shooters. We were much damaged by these and I was pulsed to know where their bullets came from for some time. On discovering I ordered a few men to fire from the second story of the house from which they successfully resisted. These Sharp Shooters, however, shot with great precision. One man near me was hit square in the fore head, the ball passing entirely through his head and wounding a man behind him severely.

The enemy were not long in forming again. This time they charged from three sides but we were ready for them and distributed the men so as to meet them on every side. They charged up near us, fired their pieces and retired, formed again and recharged. At the same time their Sharp Shooters were firing from everything that would afford them shelter. Many of our men were wounded but our loss was nothing compaired with theirs. Our fire being from the ground was much more correct than theirs and more than that our guns were much longer range. Their wounded clung to their horses to a great extent and were carried back. They found some of their dead two and three miles from the battle ground. Many of the enemy were shot as they retreated back before they got out of range of our guns. After the fight continued for some time they gave it up apparently but there were some rebels in our rear immediately between us and the main army and I was sent out with 15 of Co. A to drive them out. This we soon accomplished as Cavalry is nearly useless opposed to infantry in the wood.

We were about returning to our old position when we discovered some rebels in the road between us and the main Brigade. We opened fire on them and they raised the white flag. We could see but part of them owing to the road being washed out. When we climbed the fence we were not a little surprised to find some 40 of them. I was on the fence when I discovered this and my first thought was that they had raised a white flag for a trick and I thought to order my men back but this would not do. In fact it was too late. So shouting to them to throw down their arms we rushed over the fence and our 15 men was among their 40. Some of them hesitated about giving up their arms but a little use of our bayonets soon brought them to it and we marched them off in triumph for the Brigade that was fighting.

Arriving near them I saw a portion of them watching us suspiciously and were ready to fire upon us there being so many more of the Rebels than of our men. We looked as if we might be a body of Butternuts who had flanked them. I swong my handkerchief and we were permitted to approach. While we had been out, the command we had left had again been attacked and they were fighting hard until the whipping of the main force of the rebels put an end to the strife.

Of the main battle I am but illy posted. It appears that the rebels attacked them in the position where I left them but that our forces repulsed them and advanced to a new position nearer the enemy. This was the third position our forces had taken. The last one was along a road inclosed by two stout rail fences. In front of them was an open field about 1000 yards across bound on the opposite side by some elevated ground on which the enemy planted their guns, 8 in number. Back of our forces was woods which extended to where our little Train guard was fighting. On our right was a slightly elevated wooded position on which our three guns were planted.

The enemy having been repulsed once did not attempt another charge but opened with artillery, planting their whole 8 pieces not more than 600 or 800 yards in front of where Col. Dunnum's brigade was lying behind the fence. In fact, their guns were so close that our men of the 39th Iowa, having long range rifles, actually silenced one of their guns with them. The Enemy planted it on a knowl directly in our front and our front and our regiment opened such a fire on it that the enemy were able to fire it only once. Their horses and men were all killed or driven away before they could use it more than that.

In the mean time, the rest of their artillery was well served and with effect while our own battery was very badly managed. This state of things was rather hard to bear; to lay under such a heavy fire and be able to give the enemy nothing back. While there, it was discovered that a small party of the enemy were in the rear of the right of our force about to attack. Col. Dunnum sent orders to Col. Cummings to rally his command to the rear but Col. Cummings was dismounted and had a friendly tree between him and the enemies shell, or as he himself explained it, he had taken a tree by the left flank, but I think it was entirely a movement on the Tree's rear. I have heard some of our men and officers remark rather bitterly upon the difference, rather the contrast, of his conduct and that of the other Regimental Commanders who were mounted and in full view of the enemy. The Brigade Commander particularly rode in front of our, his command, between the fires most fearlessly.

But I was saying that the currier who brought the order to Col. Cummings was unable to find him. Consequently he shouted the command an order, "Rally to the rear," so that the whole regiment heard. I have no doubt had it been properly delivered to Col. Cummings he could have faced his Command by the rear flank and thus avoided a disgraceful confusion. As it was, the Regiment commended to execute the order as best they knew how and as soon as they got up from behind the fence for this purpose, they were exposed to the shells of the enemy (which were coming thick and fast) without any protection and without knowing perfectly what was required for them; one followed another until the whole were

in motion towards the rear about as much fleeing from the shell
of the enemy in front as persuing him in the rear. The enemy in
the rear got out of their way in very commendable time but our
regiment could not be rallied until they had run nearly one half
mile, except Companies F & D, the Co.'s on the write, who remained
and joined with a Regiment on their Right being entirely detached
from the remainder of the Regiment. Thus the line was broken and
they fell back and our Artillery fell into the hands of the Enemy.
As the horses were nearly all killed and the guns disabled, we were
unable to bring it with us.

At this juncture the Enemy sent in a flag of truce and demanded
a surrender but Col. Dunnum could not see things in that light. The
officer said he was one of Gen. Forest's Aids, that they had us all
surrounded and demanded that he surrender but Col. Dunnum told
him to go to h—l and General Forest with him. As he was parlying,
the Rebel officers regiment was seen just turning on the road to
charge us. Col. Dunnum turned to him and accused him of attacking
us under a flag of truce and presented a revolver at his head and
told him to order that regiment back or he would shoot him in a
moment. The Rebel Officer motioned them back, but about this
time the other brigade of our forces came up and attacked them in
the rear and took this regiment Prisoners and 7 pieces of cannon.

The rebels did no fighting after the second brigade come up but
commenced to skydaddle about as fast as they could to get away.
It was then about 5 o'clock I think, and the skired Rebels traveled
about 20 miles before they stopped to get supper or camp but our
forces did not persue. I cannot for the life of me tell why unless
General Sullivan is drunk. He sent out a little Cavalry, perhaps 100
men, who ran into the rear guard of the enemy and were badly cut
up. There was no infantry support near and they had to loose many
of their horses and some of their men. Had the cavalry been properly
supported by an infantry force which was at hand we could not have
helped capturing a large part of the enemies Train and many of
their horses as several regiments of them had dismounted and were
acting as suport for their artillery. Here we were camped and the
enemy of making off carrying these things with them. The Enemy
captured two or three of our old waggons which had in them large
numbers of our knapsacks. I am to night without a blanket. I expect
some infernal Rebel is enjoying mine. Our waggons were ordered
off by the acting Brigade QM who with the teams were captured. I
think, however, only about five teams were captured.

We have lost from our company a number of good men wounded.
Lieut. Rawls was slightly wounded and I have been relieved from
the Quartermaster duties to take charge of our company. The boys
are foraging sweet potatoes, ham, and whatever they can find. Col.

Dunnum is surely awful drunk to night what ever he has been today.

I have just returned from a fruitless search for our lost knapsascks. We have taken about 400 prisoners, 7 pieces of artillery, and about 1000 stand of Small Arms and about 500 horses. A splendid victory, I think, considering it was done by about one fifth of the enemies number. It is now twelve o'clock and some of the men are up cooking. It is difficult to tell if they are most in want of sleep or food.[19]

Lebanon, Kentucky

Col. W. A. Haskins awaited Morgan's attack that morning. Haskins had placed his men in a strong defensive position along the banks of Cartwright's Creek with one flank resting on a bluff and the other supported by artillery. Surely, he had blocked Morgan, who would have to fight, giving Haskins the glory of stopping and destroying the raiders. Haskins sent out a reconnaissance party of men from the Sixth Kentucky Cavalry, and they reported that the Confederates had advanced two miles toward the waiting Yankees.

No attack came. At 7:00 a.m., Haskins sent another scouting party from the Sixth, this time commanded by its colonel, Dennis J. Halisy. At 11:00, Halisy reported that the Confederate bivouac had been deserted. This timid probe prevented any effective pursuit. Still, Haskins ordered an advance in the direction of Springfield.[20]

Rolling Fork River, near Lebanon, Kentucky

Morgan and his men had made the best time they could in slipping past the U.S. position at Lebanon, but the storm that had raged all night had slowed their pace. By daybreak, they were about two and a half miles from Lebanon and eight miles from Springfield.[21]

Three men rode fast to catch up with Morgan. Morgan had sent Capt. Alexander Tribble, Lieut. George B. Eastin, and an unnamed enlisted man to the village of New Market for the purpose of seizing a supply of shoes. On their return, members of the Sixth Kentucky had spotted them and were chasing them. Then, the three officers had an opportunity to display the spirit of the "Cavalier legend" that still lingers about Confederate cavalrymen.

As the three gray horsemen came to the end of a long, straight stretch of road, they looked back and saw that all but three of their blue pursuers had given up the chase. Since they were evenly matched in numbers, they decided to take the first chance to raise the stakes and attack. When they reached the ford on the

Rolling Fork River, Eastin entered the water and reigned in his horse, turning to one side so that he was hidden by the steep bank from anyone coming into the ford. Tribble rode half-way across the stream and stopped his horse in the two-foot-deep water. The enlisted soldier did not stop at all.

Col. Dennis Halisy was the first of the pursuers to enter the river, about fifty yards ahead of his comrades. As he approached Eastin, each man fired his pistol, and each missed his target. Halisy threw up his hands, but when Eastin came toward him, the Union colonel fired again. He missed. Eastin's shot hit Halisy in the head.

By this time, the second of the U.S. troopers had engaged Tribble. Both had fired and missed, so Tribble grappled his opponent and both men went into the water, Tribble on top. With that advantage, the Yank soon gave up the fight. When the third blue-clad horseman rode up, he surrendered on the spot without a fight.[22]

Morgan's command crossed the Green River and burned a vacant stockade as well as a large amount of corn. The soldiers destroyed the bridge as soon as the rearguard had crossed.[23]

Murfreesboro, Tennessee

Sometime in the early hours of the morning, Wheeler's men began to make contact with members of Wharton's cavalry who were guarding the left flank of the Army of Tennessee. As soon as he was able to do so, Wheeler sought out Bragg's headquarters to report his success.[24]

Along the Franklin Road, outside Murfreesboro, Tennessee

The last hours of the cold darkness were slipping away, but all remained quiet. It was Bragg's intention to move at daybreak, swinging his left wing to smash Rosecrans's right, driving the Army of the Cumberland away from its line of supply and retreat, the Nashville Pike, pinning the Yankees against Stones River and Bragg's right wing.

Rosecrans was planning to strike with his left, crashing into Murfreesboro and then demolishing Bragg's left. Rosecrans allowed his men time to light fires and to cook breakfast. Bragg sent his men in hungry—time enough for breakfast after the Yanks had been whipped. Just before 6:30 a.m., Union soldiers saw dim figures looming out of the mist that hugged the ground. As the pickets guarding the U.S.

front watched, the dim figures became better defined. A solid wall of gray marched toward the unprepared Union right. Many decided it was time to retreat hastily, and they did not wait for orders.

Headquarters, Wharton's Cavalry

Gen. William Hardee personally had ordered Wharton to reach the rear of the U.S. right wing and to do all the damage he could. Wharton was making a concentrated effort, but their Confederate infantry counterparts were making their task difficult—they were driving the Yanks so fast that the horsemen couldn't catch them! "So vigorous was the attack of our left upon the enemy's right, proceeding first at a trot, then at a gallop, I had to travel a distance of 2½ miles before I reached the enemy's rear."[25] As he reached an appropriate position, Wharton ordered White's Battery to open fire against the U.S. troops in sight and soon gave the order for part of the command to charge the broken lines falling back in front of the cavalry. The result of this charge was the wholesale capture of the Seventy-Fifth Illinois Infantry.[26] Included in the prisoners was Brig. Benjamin Kirk. This unfortunate officer had been wounded and was being taken to the rear in an ambulance when overrun by the Confederate cavalry. Wharton further noted: "About this time Captain S. P. Christian, Company K, Eighth Texas Cavalry, with four companies of Texas Rangers, charged a four gun battery and captured it, including horses, drivers, harness, and everything belonging to it."[27]

Across the fields, moving toward the Nashville Pike, Wharton saw a tempting sight—the wagon train of McCook's Corps. From the markings painted on the wagon covers, he could tell that several dozen of the wagons contained ammunition. Wharton moved forward to within twelve hundred yards of the wagons, sent White's Battery into position, and put his men into line to charge. This time, the Yanks struck first. A portion of the Fourth Regular Cavalry went into formation to make a saber charge against the Texas Rangers.

One of the Rangers later recalled: "Colonel Harrison said, 'Now, boys, we will have some fun. There is a regiment out there preparing to charge us with sabers. Let them come nearly close enough to strike with them and then feed them buckshot.' The Yankee cavalry charged and we stood our ground which caused them to run within a few steps of us and stop. At that moment we fired. We asked the prisoners, 'Why did you stop? Is a saber a long-range weapon?' 'How can you kill anybody with one of them things?'"[28]

Yet more "fun" was about to befall the Texas Rangers. Their commander assigned a detail of the men to lead a party of prisoners, one of whom wore the insignia of a brigadier, to the rear. Some interrogation revealed the prisoner to be Joseph Willich, a man the Rangers had met in 1861 in a skirmish in Kentucky. In that engagement, the original commander of the Eighth Texas, Frank Terry, had been killed. Now the tables were turned.[29]

Wharton did not have all of the luck, however. As he advanced, Zahm's brigade moved into a blocking position along with four more companies of the Fourth U.S. Regulars. The ensuing clash saw the Regulars have some success in stopping part of the Confederate attack, but the rest of the U.S. force was sent into retreat. This produced a curious situation. Thomas's Corps's wagon train was open to Wharton's attack, as was McCook's. However, the U.S. cavalry that had retreated toward Murfreesboro was rallying and being reinforced. The blue troops that had been forced back toward Nashville were about to return to the field, and, during these developments, Wharton's men were scattered about the field, chasing wagons and securing prisoners. To further complicate the situation, the successful elements of the Fourth Regulars threatened White's Battery.

Wharton took his Escort Company and personally went to defend the battery. He was successful in doing this, but while he was doing so, the Union soldiers in the direction of Murfreesboro completed their reorganization and attacked from the east. Prisoners, guns, and wagons changed hands again as both sides adjusted to the changed circumstances.[30]

Rosecrans's Headquarters, Stones River Battlefield, Tennessee

During the Union counterattack along the Nashville Pike, U.S. Capt. Gates P. Thurston had extracted seventy-one of the seventy-six ammunition wagons of McCook's train and had led them towards Murfreesboro. He found a safe place for them near the left of the army (McCook originally had been on the right), and then reported to an officer on Rosecrans's staff. Soon Rosecrans himself rode up.

"Are you the officer who says McCook's ammunition train was saved?" queried the general.

Thurston saluted, "Yes, sir."

"How do you know it?"

"I had charge of it, sir."

"Where is it?" Thurston pointed out the wagons.

"How did you manage to get it way over here?"

"Well, General, we did some sharp fighting and a lot of running."

Rosecrans gave Thurston a battlefield promotion to major and made him part of Rosecrans's staff.[31] He had escaped capture by Wharton, but Thurston was already a Rebel captive. While stationed in Nashville, he had met Miss Ida Hamilton, daughter of a prominent family. The two had fallen in love and were married in 1865, two days after Thurston left the army. Thurston spent the rest of his life in Tennessee, practicing law, serving on the Nashville School Board, and serving as a member of the First Presbyterian Church. Today, he is remembered as the first collector and cataloger of Native American artifacts from Tennessee.

Left Flank, Confederate Army

Wharton had fallen back from his attack on the U.S. wagon trains about noon, bringing with him both booty and prisoners. He had turned everything and everyone over to the Provost Marshal, rested his men, fed his horses, and, in the late afternoon, led his men back toward the Union flank and rear. Wharton and his men skirmished for the rest of the afternoon.

Asbury Church, on the Nashville Pike

Wheeler had allowed his command all the rest he could, but in the afternoon he heard of a U.S. cavalry concentration that threatened the Confederate left near the Asbury Church. Moving toward the church, he and his men began to skirmish, but the sinking sun halted any definitive action.

U.S. Provost Marshal, POW Corral, Murfreesboro, Tennessee

Alexander S. McCollum, C Company, Second Georgia Cavalry, was not a happy man, and he had not had a good day. The Second Georgia had been in Murfreesboro on July 13, 1862, as part of Forrest's Birthday Raid, and that had been a much better occasion. Now, McCollum had been captured by the Third Ohio Cavalry. He had spent the day sandwiched between the collapsing Union lines and the chaos in the rear of the army. He, and the other prisoners, had been part of the rout caused by Wharton's attack on the wagon trains. He related,

> The prisoners were put to a double-quick for safer land, and the wagon train stampeded in the same direction. Just before us lay a railroad, and when the excited mules, four to each wagon, reached the railroad and the wagon wheels struck the iron rails, the wheels skidded, and the mules were thrown into the ditch. The stampede was something worth while, and as I remember it eclipsed my fear of the Confederate bullets as they passed, some of them seeming to whisper while others went screaming through. The wagon whips were popping, every teamster shouting to his mules, and the mules straining every muscle, and when they went into the ditch the teamsters went with them, and unsaddled, lay on the ground. The wagons were quickly righted up by other help and the mules thrown back in place, and no questions asked as to whether they were hurt, and no first aid was given. It was a cyclone time. We were soon halted on account of the heavy firing, for the Confederate cavalry in the rear of Rosecrans' army were burning up his wagon trains, and we had to right about face; and so we were held in full view of the battle until the fight was over. We had not been fed and when anyone mentioned the matter we were told in language never seen in a prayer book nor heard in a Sunday School, that our cavalry had burned everything.
>
> In marching through a sedge field we came upon a place where a sheep had been butchered and the head was still lying there and we did not know how long it had been there. A prisoner picked it up and said he would make a Texas dish of it. Our spirits soon rose when we saw a wagon load of corn in the rear unloading, and was guarded by soldiers with fixed bayonets. We were now in number about twelve hundred prisoners. We were marched by the corn pile and each prisoner was given two ears of corn. Only one prisoner made word of complaint. He told the Yankees they did not know how to feed up; that we ought to have a bundle of fodder to every two men (standard ration issue for a horse). Anyhow, we parched our corn; and the picture of two aged citizens held as prisoners pro-temp has never passed from my memory. They could have made the same progress with their eating had they been trying to chew buckshot. The prisoners would place their parched corn on a flat rock and scrub it with another flat rock and then lick the lower rock; thus replenishing the stock of sand we had in our gizzards.[32]

McCollum would spend several months in a Prisoner of War camp until his exchange and return to duty.

Thursday, January 1, 1863

Near Clifton, Tennessee

Forrest had left Lexington very early, because he knew that he would need time to get his men and their captured goods across the Tennessee River. Shortly after sunrise, the advance guard of the Confederate force encountered the pickets of the Sixth Tennessee Cavalry, U.S. This regiment of West Tennessee Unionists had been organized in August 1862 under the command of Col. Fielding Hurst, a prominent slave owner of the region. The Sixth Tennessee would become infamous among Confederate partisans as the war continued, but on this day Lt. Col. William K. M. Breckenridge commanded a staunch force of Union soldiers.

The pickets falling back on the main U.S. position told Breckenridge that he faced Forrest's entire force. This was a gross overestimate, as only Dibrell's regiment was on the field, but Breckenridge decided to retreat. He ordered his command to form a column by companies and then began to withdraw the rear unit, leapfrogging it to the front of the column and then having the next fall back. This was a strategic plan for a fighting retreat, since it allowed a withdrawal while keeping an organized fighting force in the rear.

Dibrell knew that he had to clear the road in a hurry if he were to keep Forrest happy, and since he feared Forrest more than he did the galvanized Yankees of the Sixth Tennessee, he ordered a charge as soon as he saw Breckenridge's tactic. The result was a Union stampede going downriver toward Decaturville. The Confederates continued south, heading up the Tennessee toward Clifton.[1]

Columbia, Kentucky

John Hunt Morgan was in a good mood. He was well on his way home, and the pursuit was falling behind. The main part of the command reached Columbia by three in the afternoon, which allowed the horses to have a good feed and the men to have a few hours' rest.

Champ Ferguson, the famous Confederate partisan from the border region of Tennessee and Kentucky, had fought with Morgan on the raid, but at Columbia, he and his men left the main column for several hours. They rode to Adair County to the house of Elam Huddleton, a man who had earned quite a reputation as a Unionist guerrilla leader. Moses and David Huddleton were in the house with Elam. Arriving in the middle of the night, the raiders opened fire on the windows of the house. The three men inside returned fire. After about an hour, Elam was wounded and the other two surrendered. Elam's brothers carried his dying body outdoors, and Ferguson shot him. Following this, Ferguson led his men to the residence of a Captain Dowdy, where they killed two brothers, Peter and Allen Zachery, both members of the Huddleton guerrilla gang. Ferguson then rejoined Morgan's column.[2]

Green River, Kentucky

The U.S. pursuit of Morgan reached Campbellsville and captured a few men who had been left behind to destroy commissary goods abandoned by U.S. forces. From these prisoners, Union officers determined that Morgan had moved toward Green River some five hours earlier. U.S. Colonel Hoskins knew that a good deal of forage had been collected at the bridge over the river, and he hoped that Morgan, once he had captured the supplies, would halt to feed his stock, thus allowing Hoskins to catch up with the raiders. He ordered two companies with a section of artillery forward at the double, but when they arrived at the river, all they found were the ruins of the bridge. Hoskins, in a determined attempt to catch Morgan, had the bridge repaired and sent his cavalry across at ten o'clock that night. The soldiers had orders to go all the way to Columbia to observe Morgan's actions.[3]

La Vergne, Tennessee

During the night of December 31, Rosecrans organized wagon trains to haul wounded men back to Nashville. A large collection of ambulances and wagons left the battlefield at 4:00 a.m. and another at 9:00 a.m. Selected companies from the Third Ohio and Fifteenth Pennsylvania, under the direction of Colonel Zahm, guarded each trip. Other wagons had left from the vicinity of Stewarts Creek. The wagons under Colonel Zahm reached La Vergne without incident and were parked along the Nashville Pike, resting both men and animals, when they spotted Confederates approaching from the direction of the battlefield.

Wheeler had spotted the detachment that had left Stewarts Creek and pursued it. As he closed in on those wagons, the much larger prize at LaVergne came into view. He ordered Wharton to take his command and deal with the smaller wagon train while Wheeler led his and Buford's command against the larger target.

Wharton soon overran the thirty or so targeted wagons, dispersing the Second Tennessee Cavalry, U.S., and capturing members of the Twenty-Second Indiana infantry. Then, Wharton hit a snag in the form of the First Michigan Engineers, who had taken shelter in a thicket of red cedar trees. Even after calling up a section of White's Battery and battering the thicket for several hours, the Michigan troops continued to hold out. Wharton never got into the fight against Zahm's wagons.[4]

While Zahm fought a rearguard action against part of Wheeler's men, the remainder of the Confederate cavalrymen rode along a parallel track, hoping to position themselves between Zahm's blocking force and the wagon train. Thrust and counter-thrust continued all afternoon until the wagons were close to Nashville and the likelihood of U.S. reinforcements became so great that Wheeler felt it prudent to withdraw.

Where Wheeler had been successful, havoc reigned. One Union officer described the scene south of La Vergne: "Teamsters had abandoned their wagons and came back mounted on their mules and horses; wagons were packed across the road, and many capsized on the side of the pike; horses ran wild through the woods, and, although men were allowed by me to pass as wagon guards, there were none at their posts. They had left the road and were bivouacking in small parties in the woods, evidently careless of the fate of the trains."[5]

Darkness found U.S. forces retreating along the Nashville Pike both toward Nashville and toward Murfreesboro. Wheeler was sandwiched in the middle, riding east to circle the Union flank and rejoin the Army of Tennessee. Wheeler reached friendly lines at about 2:00 a.m. the following morning. The fighting on January 1 had not been a great success for the Confederate cavalry. Fatigue was taking its toll, and the combat efficiency of both men and animals was declining. Rosecrans was reinforcing his convoys with infantry, and, though moving more slowly, the additional protection was effective.

Clifton, Tennessee

Col. George Dibrell led the men of the Eighth Tennessee Cavalry onto the bank of the Tennessee River across from Clifton. When their presence was confirmed with a shout, men took the two little flatboats, which had been left under the command of Capt. J. M. Barnes and Lt. Col. F. H. Daugherty, and crossed the stream to begin ferrying men and guns across. Confederate troops established a defensive position on the U.S. side of the river and placed artillery at Clifton to cover the ferry crossing.[6]

Lexington, Tennessee

Lieutenant Ayers was not a happy soldier. He complained that New Year's Day had been a miserable one, with the possible results of a victory being frittered away. He complained in his journal that the command had not marched from Parker's Crossroads until almost noon and that they walked only ten miles, having stopped at Lexington. He had heard camp rumors—which were true—that Forrest was crossing the Tennessee to safety. Ayers noted, "This looked but little like trying to catch the enemy."[7]

Friday, January 2, 1863

Clifton, Tennessee

All day long, the two small flatboats plied back and forth across the swollen Tennessee River, ferrying Forrest's men and horses to the friendly side of the river. The current was their only foe that day, as U.S. forces were conspicuous only in their absence. Morton's guns and another regiment built breastworks on a hill a mile or so inland from the ferry landing on the west bank of the river to provide a defense should any Yankees appear. Freeman positioned his guns both above and below Clifton to challenge any gunboats, but no enemy came by land or by water. No one regretted the lack of combat. John Allan Wyeth described the scene: "The men poled and rowed the boats upstream from Clifton toward the town, then out into the river so that the current swept them back downstream (north). It was the duty of the steersman to bring the boat to the Clifton side of the river. While the men were crossing two men in a canoe led a horse out into deep water where the animal had to swim, then the other horses were driven over the riverbank into the water. With the example of the swimming horse in front of them the rest followed. At one time over a thousand horses were swimming the 300 yard wide river."

Some distance to the north, General Sullivan led his U.S. troops back to Jackson, Tennessee, while Colonel Lawler proceeded a short distance farther toward Clifton. Being told by escaped Union prisoners that Forrest already was crossing the river, he, too, abandoned the pursuit.[1]

Burkesville, Kentucky

Morgan had left Columbia, Kentucky, during the night of January 1 and had reached Burkesville on the morning of the January 2. With no pursuit in sight, he allowed his men and horses to rest for some hours. Then, he crossed his command over the Cumberland River with no opposition of any kind. Some men of the advance guard said that they could hear the roar of artillery to the south.[2]

Murfreesboro, Tennessee

Wheeler's infantry and cavalry were exhausted, and their horses were in a similar condition. Days of skirmishing prior to the beginning of the battle and forty-eight hours of riding in the rear of the Army of the Cumberland had worn then out. The command did not reach Confederate lines until 2 a.m., and before they could ride again, they claimed several hours of rest. During the day, while they rested, the Orphan Brigade made its fatal attack on the U.S. forces that had crossed the river at McFadden's Ford.

As soon as darkness covered their movements, Wheeler led his and Buford's brigades to Wilkinson's Crossroads before turning northwest on a dirt road. Late at night, the command halted. The men and horses still required rest from their earlier efforts.[3]

Saturday, January 3, 1863

Clifton, Tennessee

Colonel Fuller led the sole pursuing U.S. brigade toward Clifton through a pouring rain. The road had long since turned to a quagmire, and men regularly lost their shoes in the seemingly bottomless mud of the track. Fuller paused when he reached the blocking position the Confederates had established, even though it was abandoned. A cavalry patrol ventured forward and reported that Forrest had long since crossed the river.

Acting as a thorough officer, Fuller sent the cavalry and the Twenty-Seventh Ohio to the banks of the river to make sure that Forrest was indeed gone. There was an alert picket at the ferry landing, and they fired a few shots before hustling into one of the flatboats, swimming their horses alongside. Confederate artillery opened from Clifton, and Fuller wisely fell back out of range and out of sight.[1]

With that, the West Tennessee Raid was over.

Smithville, Tennessee

Men from Morgan's command began to trickle into the village and to set up bivouacs as comfortable as they could make them. Once they crossed the Cumberland River, Morgan knew that all immediate danger was over, and he allowed his men to travel by easy stages to their rallying point. The general himself contacted army headquarters at Murfreesboro for further orders.[2]

History would name their just-ended expedition the Christmas Raid.

Antioch Church, near Murfreesboro, Tennessee

Wheeler had "boots and saddles" sounded before daybreak, and

151

his still-weary men climbed onto the backs of their horses for one more day of blocking the supply line of the Army of the Cumberland. Not far from Antioch Church, they captured a foraging party and then pressed on toward the Nashville Pike.

Approaching Wheeler was a train of ninety-five wagons loaded with hospital supplies and ammunition, all heavily protected by eight companies of infantry under Col. Daniel McCook and a detachment of cavalry commanded by Colonel Zahm. The U.S. supply train and Wheeler's cavalry met at Cox's Hill.

McCook led his infantry to the top of a hill and took up a defensive position before the horsemen could strike. Zahm kept the cavalry in hand in a position to protect the wagons. Wheeler's men were not prepared to attack uphill against a protected infantry position, and in any case, Zahm's reinforcements from Nashville were arriving steadily. At this tipping moment in the engagement, a courier arrived from Bragg ordering Wheeler to return to Murfreesboro— the Army of Tennessee would retreat. Wheeler had made his last strike at Rosecrans's supplies.

Wheeler's campaign did not end in a blaze of glory. Instead, it petered out in the cold and rain of a Southern winter. It did not all terminate on the same day, much less in the same place. His grand finale spread over several days and covered territory from central Mississippi to Middle and West Tennessee.

In less than one month, Forrest, Van Dorn, Wheeler, and Morgan accomplished significant damage to Union troops, plans, and morale. The accomplishments of the four generals of the Confederate raids won a lasting place in history.

Aftermath and Results

The immediate reaction of those who had fought in the various raids of December 1862 to January 1863 was to draw up lists of goods seized, men killed and wounded, miles of railroad track destroyed, and other such quantitative results. Of course, the Confederate and Union lists do not correspond, since each side tried to give the best interpretation possible of the results of the raids. The United States Army gave the lowest possible estimate of the men and material lost, while claiming to have inflicted great damage on the marauding Confederates. The Confederates minimized their own casualties and maximized their estimates of the goods and men they had captured. While the individual Confederate soldiers did benefit from the capture of weapons, supplies, and ammunition, these material goods did not have a long-range effect on the progress of the war. It did, however, create a feeling of accomplishment to reflect on what had been seized from the Yankees—it was good for morale throughout the Confederacy. Rev. J. N. Hunter, one of those who rode with Forrest as a young man, recalled that "the raid of two weeks may be summed up as follows: Three battles—Lexington, Trenton, and Parker's Crossroads—and innumerable skirmishes, many bridges destroyed, twenty stockades captured and burned, twenty-five hundred of the enemy killed and captured, ten pieces of artillery and fifty wagons and teams, ten thousand small arms, one million rounds of ammunition, and eighteen hundred blankets taken from the enemy and then the Tennessee River recrossed."[1] By 1913, the old veteran was still proud of his accomplishments and remembered them fondly. The aftermath and results of the raiding winter were much more far reaching than any account of goods captured and destroyed could indicate.

The four generals of the Confederacy had an apocalyptic effect on the grand strategy of the United States Army in the western theater of the war. Forrest, Morgan, Van Dorn, and Wheeler had created a new form of warfare, one still practiced today. They used a few hundred cavalrymen to stymie the advance of tens of thousands of enemy soldiers, they pinned in place two entire armies, and they prolonged the war by several months, enhancing the possibility of a Confederate victory. Cavalry continued to carry out its traditional duties of reconnaissance, scouting, and screening, but they also had a new role, that of a mobile strike force capable of penetrating enemy lines and wreaking havoc on essential components of any army's structure. This innovative strategy became the precursor to blitzkrieg, the tactics of shock and awe. However, December 1862 not only saw a fundamental change in the nature of warfare but also altered the careers of the major players of the war—on both sides.

Ulysses Grant withdrew to Memphis, leaving Vicksburg in Confederate hands for another six months. His retreat reawakened and invigorated Grant's critics. The withdrawal inspired Grant to work on another plan to gain complete control of the Mississippi for the North. This new plan respected the capabilities of the Confederate cavalry and subsequently took measures to not underestimate their force. With the greater part of the Southern horsemen deployed in Tennessee, Grant cautiously moved along the west bank of the Mississippi, an area devoid of Confederate cavalry, drawing supplies by water from Memphis. He engaged in the most sincere form of flattery by imitating the Confederates—Grant sent his most capable cavalry commander, Benjamin Grierson, on a raid of his own. Grierson had learned the lessons that Van Dorn had taught, so his raid achieved both tactical and strategic success. Furthermore, Grant carefully planned his successful 1863 campaign so as to avoid and then to neutralize the Rebel Raiders. In short, the Confederate strategy and skill taught Grant the lessons he needed in order to secure Union success.

William Starke Rosecrans also had to think long and hard about how to counter the hostile horse soldiers in gray. Although he had won a strategic victory at Murfreesboro, Rosecrans and the Army of the Cumberland were stuck in place. Morgan's destruction of the Louisville & Nashville prevented Rosencrans from replenishing his supplies in order to repair the damaged track and to fuel a counter-strike of Bragg's forces and strong guerrilla activity. While resupply via the Cumberland River was theoretically possible, a combination of low water and Confederate attacks on supply boats made the river a very unpredictable carrier of military goods.

Unlike Grant, Rosecrans could not find a route forward that

would avoid the Confederate cavalry. He determined that he would have to ride through them—a daunting prospect, given the poor showing of the U.S. cavalry in Tennessee and Kentucky. Rosecrans's solution was to re-equip his cavalry with superior firepower, a task that occupied about six months. Over the course of those months, Rosecrans managed to acquire a breech-loading carbine rifle and a Colt revolver for every one of his cavalry. This dramatically increased the rate of fire of the mounted arm and improved both efficiency and morale. The capstone of the rearmament was John Wilder's Brigade's acquisition Spencer repeating rifles, which transformed them into mounted infantry. The seven-shot Spencer became the most feared weapon in the arsenal of Rosecrans's mounted arm.

Although his army became increasingly more effective, Rosecrans's efforts to quench the Confederate guerrilla spirit were unsuccessful. This led to harsher measures against the civilian population under provost marshals such as Maj. Gen. Robert Milroy and Brig. Eleazar Paine. These officers arrested hundreds of civilians in Tennessee and Kentucky without charges and executed without trial.

From a wider perspective, Grant and Rosecrans already had bad blood in their working relationship, in particular with regard to the early stages of the Corinth Campaign. At the end of 1862, the two generals were also competing with each other for favor from the War Department. The next to win a major victory was likely to get the next big promotion. By the beginning of 1863, the Confederate cavalry had forced Grant to retreat and had left Rosecrans with a fruitless victory.

The Confederate generals also felt the effects of their raids. For Earl Van Dorn, his raiding campaign was redemption. His military and personal reputations had sunk to a very low level, but the two weeks of raiding that included the attack on Holly Springs transformed him into one of the great names in the Confederate pantheon. With Grant in retreat, Tennessee offered the greatest opportunity for Confederate success. Rosecrans could not advance; indeed, he could scarcely remain where he was. After his success, Van Dorn moved to Tennessee, where he commanded the Confederate cavalrymen from Mississippi in new movements, concentrating around Spring Hill, guarding Bragg's left flank, and harassing U.S. forces around Franklin, Murfreesboro, and Nashville. Van Dorn would report directly to Wheeler.

The star of Forrest's reputation was still ascending. He served briefly under Wheeler until Wheeler proved himself incapable of leading forays deep behind Union lines. Following the abortive attack on the U.S. garrison at Dover, Tennessee, in January 1863, the two men separated. Forrest won fame at Thompson's Station, Tennessee; Brentwood, Tennessee; and a dozen other small engagements in the western theater. He achieved rock star status when Col. Abel Streight convinced Rosecrans to authorize a raid behind Confederate lines in an attempt to disable the Western & Atlantic Railroad. Forrest's pursuit and capture of Streight became—and remains—the stuff of legend. By the end of 1863, Forrest would be promoted to major general, would have enhanced his reputation at Chickamauga, and would have engaged in the furious exchange with Bragg that led to Forrest's assignment of independent command in West Tennessee and Mississippi.

For John Hunt Morgan, the stars were in decline. The Christmas Raid was the apex of his career. For the rest of the winter of 1863, the efficiency of his command steadily deteriorated through purely his own fault. Morgan simply did not pay attention to the condition of his men or to having their needs met. Perhaps he was distracted by his new bride. At any rate, the steadily improving, better-armed U.S. cavalry roughly handled Morgan's men throughout the spring of 1863. By July, Morgan was badly executing the poorly planned Ohio Raid, wrecking both his command and his career.

Wheeler won great favor in Bragg's eyes and would retain that favor for the rest of Bragg's tenure of command. Wheeler built a solid reputation for performing the traditional duties of cavalry, but he never mastered the art of deep penetration behind enemy lines. The techniques of cavalry's new role escaped him. Every future attempt Wheeler made to raid deeply behind U.S. lines ended in failure.

The December 1862 raids were the high point for Confederate cavalry in the western theater. There would be other victories— Brice's Crossroads for Forrest, the capture of the U.S. raiders around Atlanta for Wheeler—but never again would there be such a coordinated and successful campaign that yielded such profound results. In December 1862, four generals of the Confederacy rode their way into history.

Appendix A

The Horsemen of the Confederate Raids

The men who rode the raids of December 1862 ranged from seasoned veterans to the rawest of recruits. Some of them remained under their commanders for most of the war, while others found themselves following new leaders. Who were they, these horsemen, and what else did they do during the war?

Forrest's Command

Nathan Bedford Forrest's command was quite diverse. It included troops from Tennessee, Alabama, and Kentucky. Some of them had ridden with Forrest for months, others for only days.[1] It was organized into a single brigade, although Forrest often sent regiments on detached duty in order to attack targets over a wide area.

Fourth Tennessee Cavalry (Starnes)

One of the regiments that had been with Forrest for some time was the Fourth Tennessee Cavalry. It was commanded by James Wellborn Starnes, a medical doctor and planter from Williamson County, Tennessee. Starnes had a taste for the military life, having gone to Mexico with the First Tennessee as their surgeon during the Mexican-American War. Starnes fast became a trusted subordinate of Forrest and was often be entrusted with the command of a brigade.[2] The regiment followed the regulation table of organization with ten companies:

Company A, Capt. Peril C. Haynes, men from Marshall County

Company B, Capt. John R. Davis, men from Wilson County

Company C, Capt. James M. Phillips, men from Wilson County

Company D, Capt. Delliston S. McCullough, men from Marshall and Bedford Counties

Company E, Capt. George W. Robinson, men from Coffee, Bedford, and Rutherford Counties

Company F, Capt. William Sugars McLemore, men from
  Williamson County
Company G, Capt. Andrew McGregor, men from Wilson and
  Smith Counties
Company H, Capt. Peter T. Rankin, men from Marion County
Company I, Capt. Pryor N. Harris, men from Coffee and
  Bedford Counties
Company K, Capt. Francisco Rice, men from Franklin County
  and some from north Alabama[2]

First recruited as a battalion, the unit was increased to
regimental strength in May 1862. Originally designated the Third
Tennessee, the regiment spent the first months of the war in East
Tennessee but came to Middle Tennessee to oppose the advance of
Gen. Don Carlos Buell following the Battle of Shiloh. When Bragg
led the Confederate army into Kentucky in the fall of 1862, the
regiment, now designated the Fourth Tennessee, joined Forrest
near Nashville. The regiment stayed with Forrest for the West
Tennessee Raid, Thompson's Station, Brentwood, the capture of
Streight's raiders, and the Tullahoma Campaign. During a skirmish
near Tullahoma, Colonel Starnes was mortally wounded and
replaced by William Sugars McLemore.

Colonel McLemore led the regiment at Chickamauga and then
into East Tennessee as part of Longstreet's attack on Knoxville.
In the opening phase of the Atlanta Campaign, the regiment was
part of the Army of Tennessee. When Wheeler moved north to
raid Sherman's line of supply, the Fourth divided in two. Part of
the men went with Col. George Dibrell to the Sparta, Tennessee,
area to gather recruits. This detachment was cut off from the main
army and did not rejoin it until early 1865. It fought at Saltville,
Virginia, in October 1864.

Four companies under McLemore remained with Wheeler
until the raiding force crossed the Tennessee River. At that point,
McLemore joined Forrest in Mississippi and participated in his raid
into Middle Tennessee, the Johnsonville Raid, and the Nashville
Campaign. In February 1865, the two wings of the regiment were
reunited at Grahamsville, South Carolina. The Fourth surrendered
at Greensboro, North Carolina, in April 1865.[3]

Eighth Tennessee Cavalry

Col. George Gibbs Dibrell was a successful officer who lacked
a proper military education. A merchant and farmer from Sparta,
Tennessee, Dibrell opposed secession and served as a Union delegate

to the state convention that debated the Tennessee's decision. In order to protect his home and family, he enlisted as a private when Tennessee declared its independence, became an infantry officer, and, a year later, raised a regiment of cavalry.[4] Originally given the designation of the Thirteenth Tennessee, the regiment was known in the field as the Eighth Tennessee. It had twelve companies:

Company A, Capt. W. W. Windle, men from Overton County
Company B, Capt. Hamilton McGinnis, men from Overton County
Company C, Capt. Isaac Woolsey, men from Putnam County
Company D, Capt. Jefferson Leftwich, men from White County
Company E, Capt. John S. Roberts, men from Overton County
Company F, Capt. Joseph H. Bilbrey, men from Overton County
Company G, Capt. Mounce L. Gore, men from Jackson County
Company H, Capt. James M. Barnes, men from White County
Company I, Capt. James W. McReynolds, men from White County
Company K, Capt. Bryant M. Swearingen, men from White County
Company L, Capt. James M. Barton, joined the regiment in 1863 with previously recruited men
Company L (second so named), Capt. Henry Gibson, joined the regiment in 1864 with previously recruited men[5]

Ironically, Colonel Dibrell mustered his men to take the Oath of Allegiance to the Confederacy at Yankeetown in White County, near Sparta, Tennessee. Dibrell had recruited 940 men in the original organization, who honored him with an engraved pistol. By October 1862, the regiment had completed some light training and moved a few miles west to join Forrest near Murfreesboro. At this time, the Confederate government issued the Eighth four hundred flintlock muskets, the only weapons the men ever received from them. For the remainder of the war following the West Tennessee Raid the men equipped themselves with captured guns.

On returning from West Tennessee, the Eighth spent January and February 1863 on guard duty at Florence, Alabama, and then rejoined Forrest at Spring Hill, Tennessee. While Forrest was pursuing and capturing Streight, officers sent the Eighth on a demonstration to Corinth, Mississippi, to force U.S. troops under Gen. Grenville Dodge to abandon Florence. Following the Tullahoma Campaign, the Eighth took position near Sparta to harass Union supply lines moving toward Chattanooga. Since this was their home territory, the regiment also successfully recruited men to make up their losses.

The Eighth fought at Chickamauga and at Knoxville before joining the Army of Tennessee at Dalton in March 1864. As part of Johnston's army, the regiment fought throughout the Atlanta Campaign, reduced by losses to only 140 men by August 1864. After this fragment accompanied Wheeler in his raid against Sherman's supply line, the soldiers were allowed to break away from the main force to visit their homes. They were once again successful in recruiting and returned from the expedition with about five hundred men.

Dibrell and his men confronted Sherman in his March to the Sea and continued to oppose Sherman in the Carolinas. The Eighth formed part of the escort for Jefferson Davis as he made his way into Georgia at the close of the war.[6]

The men of the Eighth were allowed to return home as one cohesive unit, only to have their personal horses and the officer's side-arms confiscated by the U.S. provost marshal at Chattanooga. Here, the provost marshal forced Colonel Dibrell to give up the engraved pistol presented to him by the White County citizens in 1862.

Cox's Cavalry Battalion

Maj. Nicholas Nichols Cox was an attorney in western Tennessee and became major of the Second Cavalry Battalion until that unit merged with other companies to form the Sixth Tennessee. At that point, Cox was authorized to raise a battalion of partisan Rangers in Perry and Hickman Counties. The battalion operated along the east bank of the Tennessee River from the mouth of Duck River to the town of Savannah, crossing the river on raids as opportunity offered. One such raid led to the capture of Henderson, Tennessee, in November 1862. This meant that Cox was able to provide expert guides for Forrest's operations when the West Tennessee Raid began.[7] Cox's Cavalry was split into five companies:

Company A, Capt. W. H. Bass, men from Perry and Humphreys Counties

Company B, Capt. W. H. Lewis, men from Perry County

Company C, Capt. Elisha S. Stevens, men from Decatur and Humphreys Counties

Company D, Capt. B. G. Rickman, men from Perry County

Company E, Capt. I. B. Herron, men from Perry and Humphreys Counties

In addition to guiding Forrest on the first West Tennessee Raid, Cox's Battalion built the flatboats that Forrest used to cross the Tennessee River at the beginning and end of the raid. They also took part in the capture of Trenton. The battalion came to its end as an organization at Parker's Crossroads, where Cox and many of his men were captured. Once exchanged, Cox became colonel of the Tenth Tennessee Cavalry, which combined Cox's Cavalry Battalion and Napier's Cavalry Battalion.[8]

Napier's Cavalry Battalion

Thomas Alonzo Napier began the war as captain of Company I, Forty-Ninth Tennessee Infantry. He was part of the garrison at Fort Donelson and became a prisoner of war under Grant's army. On the way north to a prison camp, he escaped and made his way back to Tennessee. Napier recruited a regiment of cavalry and mustered five companies in December 1862, just in time to join Forrest on his raid. The five companies were as follows:

Company A, Capt. William DeMoss, men from Davidson County
Company B, Capt. John Minor, men from Montgomery County
Company C, Capt. W. W. Hobbs, men from Humphreys County
Company D, Capt. Thomas S. Easley, men from Hickman County
Company E, Capt. D. F. Alexander, men from Henry County

The battalion was on daily active duty for the course of the raid, but Parker's Crossroads was their only major engagement. While leading a charge against the left flank of the U.S. line, Union shots killed Napier. At the conclusion of the battle, many of his men were captured. Forrest consolidated the survivors with the survivors of Cox's Battalion to become the Tenth Tennessee Cavalry.

The Tenth fought under Forrest in the spring of 1863 during the Tullahoma Campaign and at Chickamauga. They then participated in the Knoxville Campaign before rejoining the Army of Tennessee to fight in the Atlanta Campaign. When Wheeler raided Sherman's supply line in the late summer of 1864, the Tenth remained in North Mississippi under Forrest's command. The regiment also participated in the Nashville Campaign. They surrendered at Gainesville, Alabama.[9]

John Jackson's Cavalry Company, also known as Forrest's Escort

Capt. John Jackson was an infantry officer who had been wounded at Shiloh. After he had recovered, Capt. Montgomery Little recruited him as part of his cavalry command. This company was organized for the purpose of being Nathan Bedford Forrest's Escort Company, or bodyguard. On the death of Captain Little at Thompson's Station, John Jackson became the Escort's commanding officer.

As the security detail for General Forrest, the Escort was in combat in every major battle fought by Forrest's command. They were in daily contact with the General and his staff and remained at their post until the surrender at Gainesville in May 1865.

In 1877, the survivors of the Escort formed an association that continued to meet until 1909.[10]

Fourth Alabama Cavalry

Col. Alfred Alexander Russell was a physician in Stevenson, Alabama, when the war began. A veteran of the Mexican-American War, he served in an Alabama unit and a Tennessee battalion prior to the formation of the Fourth Alabama Cavalry in November 1862. Forrest characterized Russell as "cool in action, a man of fine judgment, temperate." Russell also was a fierce Confederate. At the end of the war, he refused to take the Oath of Allegiance and left the country, never to return. He began a new life as a coffee planter in Mexico. At the end of 1862, Forrest's original regiment, the Third Tennessee, broke up as units formed consisting of men from the same state. In the process, four companies of Alabama were consolidated with an existing battalion into the Fourth Alabama.[11] The ten companies were:

Company A, Capt. W. C. Bacot, men from Wilcox and Monroe counties
Company B, Capt. Alfred S. Truitt, men from Cherokee County
Company C, Capt. Frank B. Gurley, men from Madison County
Company D, Capt. William H. Taylor, men from several counties
Company E, Capt. Flavius J. Graham, men from Jackson County
Company F, Capt. Oliver B. Gaston, men from Madison County
Company G, Capt. Henry F. Smith, men from Jackson County
Company H, Capt. David Davidson, men from Marshall County
Company I, Capt. J. William Fennell, men from Marshall County
Company K, Capt. Joseph M. Hamrick, men from Madison County

Almost immediately following its organization, the Fourth accompanied Forrest on the West Tennessee Raid. Some of the men had fought with Forrest since he had organized his original command in 1861. On the raid, the Fourth saw considerable action, especially a Lexington, Trenton, and Parker's Crossroads. During the winter and spring months of 1862 to 1863, the regiment operated with Forrest from his base at Spring Hill, Tennessee.

Following the Tullahoma Campaign, the regiment fought at Chickamauga and then was assigned to Wheeler and Longstreet.

The regiment participated in the Atlanta Campaign until September 1864, when it was sent to join Gen. Philip Dale Roddey in defending the Tennessee Valley. In January 1865, the Fourth consolidated with the Seventh Alabama and returned to Forrest's command for the final campaign of the war in the western theater.

Famous members of the Fourth include Capt. Frank Gurley, who led a handful of men in an attack on a Union brigade that resulted in the death of U.S. Gen. Robert L. McCook. The McCook family insisted that Gurley had murdered their relative and had Gurley arrested post-war. Gurley was released on orders of Pres. Andrew Johnson.

John A. Wyeth fought as a boy in the Fourth's ranks. Post-war, he became one of the most acclaimed surgeons in the nation and is best remembered today as the author of a book detailing Forrest's life and career.[12]

Freeman's Battery

Samuel L. Freeman was a young attorney and former schoolteacher when the war began. Prior to Tennessee's secession, Freeman joined an artillery unit of ten guns drilling under the leadership of George H. Monsarrat. When the war began, however, Monsarrat was assigned to post duty because of his age, and his successor, Edward Baxter, also was assigned to post duty. Freeman then became battery commander. In September 1862, the unit moved to Middle Tennessee as part of the Confederate progress of into Kentucky, and Freeman was assigned to Forrest's command. When the West Tennessee raid began, the battery contained six guns.

The guns saw action at Trenton and Parker's Crossroads and in the cavalry at Spring Hill and Columbia in the spring of 1863. During their engagement at Franklin, on April 19, 1863, the Fourth U.S. Regular Cavalry took Freeman prisoner and killed him.

The battery remained with Forrest under Amariah L. Huggins until after the Battle of Chickamauga, when it was assigned to accompany Longstreet to Knoxville before returning to the Army of Tennessee. Freeman's Battery fought in Wheeler's command during his raid into Middle Tennessee in 1864 and then opposed Sherman on his March to the Sea.[13]

Morton's Battery

John Watson Morton was a student at the outbreak of the war and first saw service at Fort Donelson as a member of Porter's Battery. Captured and exchanged, he expressed a desire to serve with Forrest, who initially greeted him with skepticism because he appeared "a whey-faced boy." During the West Tennessee Raid, Morton proved his courage, and Forrest gave him command of guns captured from the U.S. forces. During this raid, Morton's Battery was formally organized.

Following the West Tennessee Raid, the battery was sent to Florence, Alabama, where they successfully engaged U.S. gunboats before continuing on to Spring Hill, Tennessee. The battery was involved in the pursuit of Able Streight, was in fierce combat at Chickamauga, and accompanied Forrest to Mississippi in 1864.

In May 1864, Forrest made Morton the Chief of Artillery for his command, and Lt. T. Sanders Sale took command of the battery. Under Sale, the battery was involved in all of Forrest's operations until the end of the war.

The men of this battery represented every one of the Confederate States and even part of the Union—one gunner came from Massachusetts. The battery did not lose a single gun to the enemy throughout the entire war.

Morgan's Command

John Hunt Morgan was married and promoted to brigadier only days prior to beginning his Christmas Raid. In order to facilitate his movements, Morgan divided his command into two brigades, the first led by Basil Wilson Duke and the second by William Breckinridge.

Duke's Brigade

Basil Wilson Duke was active in the secession movement in Missouri, where he practiced law when the war began. He returned to his native Kentucky and enlisted as a private in the cavalry unit organized by his brother-in-law, John Hunt Morgan. Duke served with Morgan until the Ohio Raid of 1863. When he was exchanged from prison, Duke commanded troops in eastern Kentucky and western Virginia. At the end of the war, he was part of the escort that guarded Confederate president Jefferson Davis as he moved south. Post-war, Duke was an attorney and author.[14]

Second Kentucky Cavalry

John Hunt Morgan organized a squadron of cavalry at Bowling Green, Kentucky, in October 1861. Following the Battle of Shiloh, other companies joined Morgan's command until it reached regimental size during the summer of 1862. The regiment fought under Kirby Smith during the Kentucky Campaign and became part of Wheeler's cavalry corps. When Morgan was promoted to brigadier, Duke became colonel of the regiment, but when the Christmas Raid began and Duke led a brigade, Lt. Col. John B. Hutchinson led the cavalry into Kentucky. The ten units were as follows:

Company A, Capt. John Cassell
Company B, Capt. John Allen
Company C, Capt. James Bowles
Company D, Capt. John B. Castleman
Company E (no surviving record of captain)
Company F, Capt. Thomas Webber
Company G, Capt. Robert McFarland
Company H, Capt. Gabe S. Alexander
Company I, Capt. Joseph Desha
Company K, Capt. William Jennings

Following the Christmas Raid, the regiment served with Morgan in Middle Tennessee, often confronting John Wilder's Mounted Infantry. The regiment was decimated in the Ohio Raid of 1863, and only a fragment of its number remained for active duty.[15]

Third Kentucky Cavalry

Also called the Seventh Kentucky, in December 1862, Lt. Col. J. M. Huff commanded the regiment. The regiment had first been organized and commanded by Col. Richard M. Gano, but he was on furlough at the time of the Christmas Raid. The regiment fought with Morgan until it was largely destroyed during the Ohio Raid. A remnant was reorganized in 1864 and saw service in Tennessee and Virginia until the end of the war. Some of these men were part of the escort of Jefferson Davis when he was captured.[16]

Eighth Kentucky Cavalry

Col. Leroy Stuart Cluke, a veteran of the Mexican-American War, was a well-known horse trader prior to the war. The organizer of the Eighth Kentucky Cavalry, he was a bold leader. Captured on the Ohio Raid, he died of disease at Johnston's Island Depot of Prisoners of War.[17]

Palmer's Battery

The battery was organized as the Southern Rights Battery in Houston County, Georgia, in March 1862, in which most of the officers and sergeants were veterans of the First Georgia Infantry.

The battery was part of the Fourteenth Battalion, Georgia Light Artillery, and became one of the best trained artillery units in the Army of Tennessee. They fought at Perryville before being mounted as horse artillery and being assigned to accompany Morgan on the Christmas Raid. Following the raid, Capt. Joseph Palmer was promoted to major and M. H. Havis became the commanding captain of the unit.

Dismounted, the battery served as part of the Reserve Artillery Battalion of the Army of Tennessee, seeing action during the Tullahoma Campaign, at Chickamauga, at Missionary Ridge, on the Atlanta Campaign, and at Macon Arsenal. Returning to field duty in the spring of 1865, the battery surrendered at Greensboro, North Carolina, in April of that year.[18]

Breckinridge's Brigade

William Campbell Preston Breckinridge came from a Unionist family but followed his cousins into the Confederate service. He helped raise the Ninth Kentucky Cavalry but often served as temporary commander of a brigade. He surrendered at Augusta, Georgia, in May 1865, and returned to Kentucky to become a newspaper editor and U.S. Congressman.[19]

Initially, Morgan offered command of the brigade to Adam R. Johnson, the senior of the regimental commanders, but he waived his right to the position, so he offered the command to Breckinridge instead.[20]

Ninth Kentucky Cavalry

William C. P. Breckinridge also was one of the organizers of this regiment, but Lt. Col. Robert G. Stoner led the unit during the Christmas Raid, as Breckinridge commanded the ad hoc brigade.

Following the Christmas Raid, the Ninth helped to defend Bragg's right flank around McMinnville before being detached from Morgan's command to remain with the main army. The regiment fought at Lookout Mountain, at Ringgold Gap, in the Atlanta Campaign, and at Saltville. In late 1864, it opposed Sherman on the March to the Sea and fought in the last major battle at Bentonville.

In the last days of the war, the remnants of the Ninth became part of the escort for Jefferson Davis. The men surrendered at Washington, Georgia, on May 10, 1865.[21]

Tenth Kentucky Cavalry, also known as Johnson's Rangers, also known as Partisan Rangers

Col. Adam Rankin Johnson had moved from Kentucky to the Texas frontier, where he made a reputation for himself as an Indian fighter. As the Civil War began, he returned east to serve as a scout for Forrest. After his capture at Fort Donelson, Johnson escaped with General Floyd. As a Partisan Ranger, he attacked and captured Newburgh, Indiana, by threatening to bombard it with two cannon (which were actually pieces of stovepipe mounted on the running gear of a wagon). He and his Rangers became the Tenth Kentucky and served with Morgan until the end of the Ohio Raid. Johnson escaped U.S. forces at that time and returned to his career as a Partisan. Wounded by his own men in 1864, he lost sight in both eyes but served on active duty for the rest of the war.[22] The Tenth was divided into eleven companies:

Company A, Capt. Montgomery Swope, men from Hopkins, McLean, and Webster Counties

Company B, Capt. William M. Marr, men from Henderson County, Kentucky, and Montgomery County, Tennessee

Company C, Capt. Sam Wall, men from Crittenden, Union, and Webster Counties

Company D, Capt. L. D. Fisher, men from Henderson County, Kentucky, and Montgomery County, Tennessee

Company D (reorganization), Capt. T. M. Hammack, men from Union County

Company E, Capt. Samuel B. Taylor, men from Daviess, Hancock, and Jefferson Counties

Company F, Capt. John S. Chapman, men from Union County

Company G, Capt. J. N. Taylor, men from Henderson County

Company H, Capt. J. N. Taylor, men from Henderson County

Company I, Capt. Alfred Fowler, men from Hopkins County

Company K, Capt. John H. Hamby, men from Caldwell, Christian, and Hopkins Counties

The Tenth Kentucky Cavalry, or Partisan Rangers, joined Morgan for the Christmas Raid following a career of small operations behind U.S. lines in Western Kentucky. The Tenth remained with Morgan during the Ohio Raid and many of its men escaped from the pursuing forces by swimming the Ohio River. In 1864, Johnson was allowed to reassemble the remnants of "Morgan's Men" and formed a small brigade that did service in eastern Kentucky and southwestern Virginia. This command surrendered in late April 1865.[23]

Eleventh Kentucky Cavalry

Col. David Waller Chenault, a veteran of the Mexican-American War, received permission during Bragg's 1862 Kentucky Campaign to form a cavalry regiment of Kentucky volunteers. He led the regiment until his death in combat on July 4, 1863, at Green River Bridge, Kentucky.[24]

Company A, Capt. Gordon C. Mullins, men from Clark County

Company B, Capt. Joseph Chenault, men from Madison County

Company C, Capt. Andrew Jackson Bruner, men from Clark County

Company D, Capt. J. N. L. Dickens, men from Estill County

Company E, Capt. Robert T. Terrill, men from Madison County

Company F, Capt. Thomas B. Collins, men from Madison County

Company G, Capt. James Mitchel, men from Bourbon County

Company H, Capt. Augustus H. McGaee, men from Madison County

Company I, Capt. Jack May, men from Estill County

Company K, Capt. B. S. Barton, men from Clinton and Wayne Counties

Formed in Kentucky while the Confederate army was there in 1862, the Eleventh saw combat on their withdrawal from that state. They later fought at Hartsville, Tennessee, and took part in the Christmas Raid. During the early spring of 1863, they were involved in several small actions on the right flank of Bragg's army. Only part of the regiment took part in the Ohio Raid, but those who did were captured and not exchanged until the war was almost over. The remnant left behind by Morgan served the rest of the war in eastern Tennessee and southwestern Virginia.[25]

Fourteenth Tennessee Cavalry

Col. James D. Bennett raised this regiment, which was known by several numerical designations, including Nine and Fifteen. When Colonel Bennett was wounded in September 1862, Col. William Walker Ward assumed command of the regiment and led it until his capture during the Ohio Raid. A lawyer, Ward had served in the Tennessee legislature prior to the war. After he was exchanged, Ward fought in East Tennessee until wounded at Bull's Gap in 1864.

Company A, Capt. Micajah Griffin, men from Sumner County

Company B, Capt. William P. Simmons, men from Sumner and Trousdale Counties

Company C, Capt. John D. Kirkpatrick, men from Sumner County

Company D, Capt. William D. Ward, then A.B. Gates, men from Smith County

Company E, Capt. Alex W. Rowe, men from Sumner and Trousdale Counties

Company F, Capt. A.E. Bell, men from Sumner County

Company G, Capt. Charles E. Cossett, men from Sumner and Smith Counties

Company H, Capt. John W. Wiseman, men from Sumner, Trousdale, and Wilson Counties

Company I, Capt. Felix H. Blackman, men from Davidson County

Company K, Capt. J. Richard McCann, men from Davidson and Rutherford Counties

This regiment skirmished in the vicinity of Nashville following its organization in September 1862 and then moved into Kentucky with Wheeler's command. They participated in the Battle of Murfreesboro in December 1862 and then accompanied Morgan on the Christmas Raid. They remained with Morgan in the spring of 1863, fighting to protect Bragg's right flank. The regiment was decimated in the Ohio Raid, but some later reached Calhoun, Georgia, and served in the First Kentucky Battalion under Basil Wilson Duke. They ended the war in southwestern Virginia.[26]

Corbett's Battery

Lt. C. C. Corbett commanded a battery of four twelve-pound mountain howitzers. No history of the unit exists, but Corbett had his photograph made in 1863 while a prisoner of war. The battery appears to have been captured on the Ohio Raid.

White's Section

Capt. Benjamin F. White Jr. commanded this battery, but only his heavy, three-inch Parrot guns were chosen to make the raid, since they provided the firepower to blast through the walls of wooden stockades and other light fortifications that guarded the railroad. The light guns of the battery were given a temporary assignment to Wharton's brigade of Wheeler's command.

Van Dorn's Command

Texas Brigade

Col. John Summerfield Griffith commanded this brigade. Griffith was born in Maryland but his family moved to Texas as pioneers.

He raised a cavalry company at the beginning of the war and rose in rank on his merit. He resigned his commission in the spring of 1863 for health reasons and returned to Texas. After the war, he was active in politics.[27]

The men of the Texas Brigade covered more territory and fought in more battles than any other Confederate unit. Raised in Texas, they began the war in Indian Territory (Oklahoma) before moving on to Missouri, Arkansas, Mississippi, Tennessee, Alabama, and Georgia. For several months after crossing the Mississippi River in 1862, they functioned as infantry before being remounted. As cavalry, they fought under Van Dorn, Wheeler, and Forrest. Major battles and campaigns in which they participated included Elkhorn Tavern, Siege of Corinth, Iuka, Battle of Corinth, Holly Springs, Thompson's Station, Vicksburg Campaign, Atlanta Campaign, Nashville Campaign, and the Selma Campaign. This was a hard-riding, hard-fighting command.

The brigade included the First Texas Legion (also called the Twenty-Seventh Texas), commanded by Capt. E. R. Hawkins; the First Texas Cavalry, commanded by Maj. J. H. Broocks; the Third Texas Cavalry, commanded by Lt. Col. Jiles S. Boggess; the Sixth Texas Cavalry, commanded by Capt. Jack Wharton; and the Ninth Texas Cavalry, commanded by Col. Dudley W. Jones. The size of these regiments steadily decreased the farther east they traveled because of the distance from their homes made recruiting difficult. The brigade is also known as Ross's Brigade, although Laurence Sullivan Ross was not in command at the time of the Holly Springs raid. Ross was its most famous and colorful commander.

The brigade surrendered with Forrest on May 26, 1865, in Gainesville, Alabama.[28]

Tennessee Brigade

Col. William Hicks Jackson commanded this unit of Van Dorn's Command.

Seventh Tennessee Cavalry

Col. John G. Stocks was a veteran of the Mexican-American War and raised a battalion of cavalry in 1861. He was promoted from lieutenant colonel in the Seventh Tennessee to colonel. He resigned in October 1863 because of a back injury.

Formed by the merger of unassigned companies and Logwood's Battalion (Sixth Tennessee Cavalry), the regiment served in the vicinity of Union City until the capture of Memphis by U.S. forces compelled its retreat from West Tennessee. The Seventh then fought at Britton's Lane and at the Siege of Corinth. In 1863, the regiment served in Mississippi and then fought under Forrest's command in 1864, at which time Col. William L. Duckworth commanded the unit. Under Forrest, the Seventh fought in all of the battles in West Tennessee and Mississippi in 1864; was part of the Nashville Campaign; fought at Tuscaloosa, Alabama; and surrendered at Gainesville, Alabama, in May 1865.[29]

First Tennessee Cavalry, also known as the Sixth Tennessee Cavalry

Col. James Thaddeus Wheeler was a veteran of the Mexican-American War living in Giles County, Tennessee, at the outbreak of the Civil War. His regiment was formed by the merger of two battalions. Wounded in the Holly Springs Raid, Wheeler later served under Forrest until his regiment also was consolidated with others. He was sent to his home in Pulaski, Tennessee, in November 1864 to recruit, and he surrendered there in 1865. Wheeler stood at an exceptional height for his day of six feet, four inches.[30]

The regiment was cut off at Corinth when Bragg evacuated. Cutting its way out, the men fought at Britton's Lane and in Mississippi before participating in the Holly Springs Raid. The unit moved to Spring Hill and then took part in the Tullahoma Campaign, Chickamauga, and the Atlanta Campaign. Part of the regiment stayed with Gen. Joseph Wheeler and fought Sherman in the March to the Sea, but Col. James Wheeler went to Middle Tennessee to recruit and left his new men to fight with Forrest in the fall and winter of 1864. The men with Colonel Wheeler were consolidated into other Tennessee regiments during the Nashville Campaign, while those with General Wheeler surrendered in North Carolina.

In October 1861, Pvt. George Barham was killed near Hopkinsville, Kentucky. Pvt. Edwards of the same company was killed on May 4, 1865. Thus, two men from this regiment were the first and last combat deaths of the Army of Tennessee.[31]

Mississippi and Missouri Brigade

This brigade fought under the direction of Col. Robert M. McCulloch.

First Mississippi Cavalry

Col. Andrew Jackson Lindsay was from Limestone County,

Alabama, but joined the Regular Confederate Army instead of accepting a commission with state troops in the Provisional Army. Lindsay was a graduate of West Point, a veteran of the Mexican-American War, and was a captain on active duty with the U.S. Mounted Riflemen when the Civil War began. Assigned to command Mississippi troops, he served in this capacity until wounded at Shiloh and then held no combat command until the end of the war.[32]

Col. R. A. Pinson was given command of the regiment and led it at the Siege of Corinth and at Britton's Lane. The First fought at the Second Battle of Corinth and then opposed Grant before participating in the Holly Springs Raid. Moving to Tennessee with Van Dorn, the regiment fought at Thompson's Station but returned to Mississippi to participate in the Vicksburg Campaign. They opposed Sherman on the Meridian Expedition and then were moved east to fight in the Atlanta Campaign. Assigned to Forrest for the Nashville Campaign, the regiment remained with him in 1865, fighting at Selma and then surrendering at Gainesville, Alabama.[33]

Second Missouri Cavalry

Col. Robert "Black Bob" McCulloch formed this regiment for the Missouri State Guard. As a battalion, they fought west of the Mississippi at Boonville, Wilson's Creek, Pea Ridge, and Lexington. Crossing the river with Sterling Price, the unit was increased in size to a regiment.

Colonel McCulloch was born in Virginia but moved west and went to California in 1849. By the time the war began, he was back in Missouri. In 1864, he led a brigade under Forrest but was never promoted to brigadier. Black Bob was wounded at Tupelo and Harrisburg but survived the war to return to Missouri. His cousin, also named Robert, served in the same regiment and was called "Red Bob" to distinguish between the two.[34] Red Bob commanded the regiment on the Holly Springs expedition.

Once on the eastern bank of the Mississippi, the Second Missouri fought at Corinth; Courtland, Alabama; and Britton's Lane. At the Battle of Corinth, the unit fought on foot. Following the Holly Springs Raid, the regiment stayed in northern Mississippi and engaged in numerous small skirmishes until the end of 1863. When Forrest took command in Mississippi, the Second became a favorite of the general's and saw combat in all of the battles of West Tennessee, including Fort Pillow, until

September 1864 when the unit was sent to Mobile. The Second returned to Forrest's command in the early months of 1865 and reported directly to Forrest instead of being assigned to a brigade. Following their final fight at Selma, the regiment surrendered at Gainesville, Alabama, in 1865.[35]

Wheeler's Command

Wheeler's command was divided into four brigades, commanded by Gen. Joseph Wheeler, Gen. John Pegram, Gen. John A. Wharton, and Gen. Abraham Buford respectively.

Wheeler's Brigade

First Alabama Cavalry

Col. James Clanton organized the regiment near Montgomery, Alabama, but was promoted, leaving Col. William W. Allen in command until he was wounded at Stones River. The regiment fought at Shiloh; Booneville, Mississippi; and in the Kentucky Campaign. Following Stones River, it took part in the Tullahoma Campaign and then fought at Chickamauga and with Gen. James Longstreet. Participation in the Atlanta Campaign included the capture of Gen. George Stoneman's cavalry. It fought in the final battle at Bentonville, North Carolina, and surrendered at Salisbury, North Carolina, with 150 men.

Third Alabama Cavalry

Maj. F. Y. Gaines commanded the regiment that was formed at Tupelo, Mississippi, in June 1862. Some of the companies from which it was formed had fought at Shiloh. The regiment was constantly engaged during the Kentucky Campaign and fought heavily at Stones River. Although it suffered many losses at Shelbyville, the regiment proceeded on to fight at Chickamauga, at Knoxville, and in the Atlanta Campaign. The Third opposed Sherman and fought at Bentonville. A skeleton of the original organization surrendered with the Army of Tennessee.

Fifty-First Alabama Cavalry

Col. John T. Morgan commanded a unit of mounted infantry organized at Oxford, Alabama, in August 1862. The Fifty-First joined Forrest near La Vergne for a brief time before transferring to Wheeler's command. Escaping from Stones River with light losses, the regiment lost almost half its force at Shelbyville. The regiment was part of the rearguard on the retreat to Chattanooga and fought at Chickamauga. It participated in the Sequatchie Raid before marching to Knoxville with Longstreet. It fought in the Atlanta Campaign, opposed Sherman, and surrendered in North Carolina.

Eighth Confederate Cavalry

Col. William Bartee Wade assumed command of the regiment when Col. Richard H. Brewer was transferred to staff duty in June 1862. The regiment was formed after the Battle of Shiloh by the consolidation of several battalions. Six of the companies came from Mississippi and four from Alabama.

The Eighth fought in the Siege of Corinth, the Kentucky Campaign, Stones River, and the Tullahoma Campaign. During the latter campaign, they lost heavily in an engagement at Shelbyville. At Chickamauga, the regiment was assigned to Forrest's command, then to Wheeler's, and finally was split with the Mississippi companies sent to Forrest and the Alabama men remaining with Wheeler.

First Tennessee Cavalry

Col. James Epps Carter organized this regiment by uniting two cavalry battalions in November 1862. Carter and most of the men in the unit were from the Knoxville area, and they first served in the vicinity of the Cumberland Gap. The regiment joined Wheeler for the Stones River campaign and was then sent to guard the far right flank of Bragg's defense line during the spring of 1863. Most of the regiment was then sent to East Tennessee, but one detachment went to Mississippi and before heading to fight in the Atlanta Campaign. This regiment did not surrender but disbanded in April 1865.[36]

Tennessee Battalion (Douglass)

Maj. DeWitt Clinton Douglass, formerly of the Seventh Tennessee Infantry, organized this unit as a partisan Ranger battalion in October 1862. It saw service under Forrest around Nashville prior to the West Tennessee Raid, at which time the battalion joined Wheeler's command. It fought under Wheeler at Stones River and then was consolidated with Holman's Tennessee Battalion to form the Eleventh Tennessee Cavalry. Some of the men did not participate in the merger and chose to join Morgan's command instead. They were captured on the Ohio Raid.[37]

Tennessee Battalion (Holman)

Maj. Daniel W. Holman, formerly of the First Tennessee Infantry (Turney's) formed this battalion in the fall of 1862. The unit reported to Wheeler on approximately December 1, 1862, and soon found itself in the opening stages of the Stones River Campaign. They then participated in the move on Dover and scouted the Cumberland River. They merged with Douglass's Tennessee Battalion to become the Eleventh Tennessee Cavalry.[38]

Gen. Forrest ordered the Eleventh to be created over the objections of the officers of both battalions. However, the regiment fought well at Thompson's Station, Day's Gap, the Tullahoma Campaign, and Chickamauga. The regiment also participated in the Atlanta Campaign. Some of the men were cut off in Tennessee during Wheeler's raid of September 1864. This part of the regiment fought at Saltville and then opposed Sherman. The main part of the regiment rejoined Forrest for the Nashville Campaign and ended the war with him at Gainesville.[39]

Wiggins's Arkansas Battery, also known as the Clark County Artillery or the Second Arkansas Light Artillery

Officially known as the Clark County Artillery or the Second Arkansas Light Artillery, this battery traces its history to May 1861, when it was organized at Arkadelphia, Arkansas. The unit spent the first several months of the war on garrison duty in Arkansas but was sent east in early 1862. Jannedens H. Wiggins became battery commander in May 1862. At about this time, the battery was assigned to service with the cavalry, and all personnel were mounted, making Wiggins's Battery a horse-artillery unit. In this capacity, the battery seldom acted as a unit but did duty as three two-gun sections.

The section under Captain Wiggins was overrun by the Seventh Pennsylvania Cavalry in a saber charge at Shelbyville, Tennessee, on June 27, 1863. Excluding a few officers, who were exchanged late in the conflict, the men of this section spent the rest of the war in prisoner of war camps. The remaining sections fought in the Atlanta Campaign and opposed Sherman on the March to the Sea. Wiggins was exchanged and rejoined the remnant of the battery in the spring of 1865. Ten men surrendered at Newton, North Carolina.

Pegram's Brigade

First Georgia Cavalry

Col. James J. Morrison, a veteran of the Mexican-American War, formed this regiment at Rome, Georgia. Once organized, the regiment reported to Chattanooga and was assigned to duty at Knoxville. On June 9, 1862, Forrest was tasked with organizing all the cavalry in the area, and the First Georgia came under his command. The unit participated in the Birthday Raid at Murfreesboro before returning to East Tennessee, where it remained until 1863 when it rejoined the Army of Tennessee to fight at Chickamauga. In this battle, Colonel Morrison was severely wounded.

After fighting with Longstreet in the Knoxville Campaign, the First saw action in the Atlanta Campaign before being detached for duty along the Atlantic Coast. They rejoined Wheeler to oppose Sherman. The regiment surrendered with the Army of Tennessee.[40]

First Louisiana Cavalry

Col. John Sims Scott organized this regiment with heavy financial support from wealthy planters, and so the regiment had an aristocratic, independent tone that often clashed between the soldiers and their brigade commanders.

The First was stationed on the north side of the Cumberland River at Fort Donelson but did not surrender there. They later became part of the rearguard during Nashville's evacuation. At Shiloh, the regiment served with Forrest on the far right Confederate flank. When Corinth was evacuated, the unit transferred to North Alabama and Middle Tennessee, where it served in an independent capacity until the Kentucky Campaign. At the Battle of Richmond, Kentucky, the regiment waited at U.S. rear and ambushed the retreating soldiers.

Back in Tennessee, the First was assigned to Wheeler during the Stones River Campaign and then followed Gen. John Pegram on a raid into Kentucky. They repeated this performance in an attempt to divert attention from Morgan's thrust north in July 1863. At the conclusion of this attempt, the regiment returned to Forrest's command.

When Forrest went to Mississippi in 1863, the First stayed with the Army of Tennessee and fought at Missionary Ridge. In the opening days of 1864, it went with Polk into western Alabama until Polk rejoined the main army, at which time the First again returned to Forrest's command. Forrest assigned the regiment to its home region, and it spent the remainder of the war engaging in various small engagements in southwest Mississippi and eastern Louisiana.

Scott had been court-martialed once in 1863 and was charged for unauthorized dealings with the enemy in 1865. He was relieved of command in March of that year. The remnants of the regiment were at Columbus, Mississippi, when the war ended.[41]

Wharton's Brigade

First Confederate Cavalry

Col. John T. Cox led this regiment for much of its career. Formed in April 1862 with men from Alabama, Kentucky, and Tennessee, the unit fought at Shiloh, in the Kentucky Campaign, at Stones River, and in the Tullahoma Campaign. The regiment was decimated at Shelbyville, and only a fragment remained to participate in the rest of the war. There are no records of rosters of this regiment for the summer of 1864, but it is mentioned as being involved in the Nashville Campaign from 1864 to 1865. There are documents stating that the First Confederate fought under Wheeler in North Carolina.

Third Confederate Cavalry

Col. William N. Estes commanded this regiment upon the resignation of its organizing officer, I. B. Howard, until Estes's death near Chattanooga. Seven of the companies were from Alabama, and three hailed from Georgia. It was always under-strength for a unit and averaged only about two hundred active soldiers at the time of Stones River.

Fourteenth Alabama Battalion

Lt. Col. James C. Malone commanded this Partisan Ranger unit of six companies. It was organized shortly before December 1862 and combined with the Nineteenth Battalion to form the Seventh Alabama Cavalry in April 1863.

Second Georgia Cavalry

The Second Georgia was raised by Col. Winburn Joseph Lawton, a planter and member of the state legislature. In the summer of 1862, the regiment was part of Forrest's newly organized brigade and took part in the Birthday Raid on Murfreesboro. Moving to East Tennessee, Col. Charles Constantine Crews replaced Lawton, and the regiment transferred to Wheeler's command.

At Stones River, Crews was wounded, and Lt. Col. J. E. Dunlop took over. In 1863, the unit fought at Dover, took part in the Tullahoma Campaign, fought at Chickamauga, served in the Atlanta Campaign, and opposed Sherman during the March to the Sea and in the Carolinas Campaign. The regiment surrendered at Charlotte, North Carolina. In sum, the Second fought in 175 engagements in Kentucky, Tennessee, Alabama, Georgia, South Carolina, and North Carolina.[42]

Third Georgia Cavalry

Maj. R. Thompson commanded the regiment at Stones River, Col. M. J. Crawford having been killed in combat earlier. The regiment mustered into service at Athens, Georgia, in the summer of 1862. It served under Wheeler at Stones River, Chickamauga, the Atlanta Campaign, and against Sherman. The unit surrendered with the Army of Tennessee.

Second Tennessee Cavalry

Col. H. M. Ashby commanded this regiment, formed by the consolidation of several battalions, in May 1862. Assigned to Gen. Edmund Kirby Smith in East Tennessee, the unit fought in the vicinity of the Cumberland Gap prior to joining Wheeler in the Stones River Campaign. In early 1863, it operated in Kentucky and eastern Tennessee before fighting at Chickamauga. The regiment fought in the Atlanta Campaign and in the Carolinas, ending the war as part of the command of Wade Hampton.

Fourth Tennessee Cavalry, also known as the Eighth Tennessee Cavalry

Col. Baxter Smith organized this regiment in September 1862 at Knoxville, combining small units that had fought in places as distant as Clinch Mountain, Virginia, and Fort Donelson. Following the Kentucky Campaign, the regiment fought at Stones River, in the Tullahoma Campaign, at Chickamauga, in the Atlanta Campaign, at Saltville, and in the Carolinas Campaign. The regiment surrendered at Charlotte, North Carolina, in May 1865.

Tennessee Regiment (Murray)

In August 1862, several companies combined with an existing battalion to form a regiment placed under the command of Col. John P. Murray. Although referenced as the Fourth Tennessee Cavalry, the numerical designation was seldom used because there were already two other regiments with that number, Starnes's and Smith's.

The regiment skirmished around Nashville before participating in the Kentucky Campaign and then the Stones River Campaign. The regiment disbanded and the men reassigned to other units in January 1863.

Tennessee Battalion (Davis)

Maj. John R. Davis formed this battalion at Bardstown, Kentucky, in September 1862. It fought in the Stones River Campaign and then consolidated into Col. Baxter Smith's Fourth Tennessee Cavalry in January 1863.

Wharton's Escort Company

Capt. Paul F. Anderson led a company informally called the "Cedar Snags" from Warren County. They were an independent company until January 1863, when they were assigned to Col. Baxter Smith. At Stones River, they served as the Escort Company for General Wharton.

Buford's Brigade

Third Kentucky Cavalry

Col. J. R. Butler organized this unit in the summer of 1861. It served in several small engagements in 1862 and was surprised in camp at Sweeden's Cove on June 4, 1862. It suffered heavily in the Kentucky Campaign. As a result, it merged with the First Kentucky Cavalry and, as such, fought at Stones River, Chickamauga, Missionary Ridge, the Atlanta Campaign, Charleston, and the Carolinas Campaign. It surrendered with the Army of Tennessee in 1865.

Fifth Kentucky Cavalry

Col. D. H. Smith organized this regiment in the summer of 1862. It fought at Stones River and then helped hold Bragg's right flank on the Cumberland Plateau before transferring to Morgan's command on the Ohio Raid. The regiment was wiped out during this operation.

Sixth Kentucky Cavalry

Col. J. W. Grigsby led this regiment from its organization in the summer of 1862 through the Stones River Campaign and until it was wiped out during the Ohio Raid under Morgan's command.

Notes

Friday, December 12, 1862
   1. McWhiney and Hallock, 140.
   2. *Official Records,* ser. 1, vol. 20, pt. 1, 64.
   3. Wyeth, *That Devil Forrest,* 90; Maness, *Lightning Warfare,* 90; Jordan and Pryor, 189; Allardice, 325, 62, 330; Warner, 72-73.
   4. Beard, "Bravest of Brave," 364.
   5. *Official Records,* ser. 1, vol. 17, pt. 2, 422.
   6. Simpson, 166-67.
   7. Hartje, 255.
   8. Rose, 131-32, 153-54; Hale, 31; Allardice, 174-75, 188, 190-91.
   9. *Official Records,* ser. 1, vol. 17, pt. 2, 466.
   10. Ballard, 109.
   11. *Official Records,* ser. 1, vol. 20, pt. 1, 77-78.

Saturday, December 13, 1862
   1. Parks, 282.
   2. West, "The President's Coming."
   3. Morton, 46.
   4. Allardice, 112.
   5. Morton, 47.
   6. Beard, "West Tennessee," 304. Clifton lies at the foot of a horseshoe bend in the Tennessee River, and the course of the river is, for a short distance, west to east. Because of this bend, Forrest was actually crossing from south to north but, since this put him on the west bank of the river, I have consistently referred to the crossing as if it were east to west.

Sunday, December 14, 1862
   1. *Official Records,* ser. 1, vol. 20, pt. 2, 449.
   2. Ibid., pt. 1, 80.
   3. West, "Wedding;" Shirley Farris Jones, "Martha Ready Morgan."
   4. *Official Records,* ser.1, vol. 17, pt. 1, 496-97.

Monday, December 15, 1862
1. Carter, 129; Hartje, 256.
2. *Official Records,* ser. 1, vol. 20, pt. 1, 83.
3. Shirley Farris Jones, "Martha Ready Morgan."
4. *Official Records,* ser. 1, vol. 20, pt. 1, 497; Cadwallader, 32. This text is treated with caution by many historians because it was not printed until many years after the war and contains assertions which cannot be verified by other sources. Cadwallader always makes himself the center of attention and a fountain of good advice for one and all. In this case, however, his account of the Dickey raid is in accord with Colonel Dickey's report in the *Official Records.*

Tuesday, December 16, 1862
1. Jordan and Pryor, 194.
2. Hartje, 257; A. F. Brown, 6:155.
3. Hyneman, 586.

Wednesday, December 17, 1862
1. Steenburn, 108; Bearss, "West Tennessee," 13.
2. *Official Records,* ser. 1, vol. 17, pt. 2, 429.
3. A. F. Brown, 6:153.
4. *Official Records,* ser. 1, vol. 17, pt. 2, 424.
5. Ibid., pt. 1, 498; Cadwallader, 33.
6. *Official Records,* ser. 1, vol. 17, pt. 1, 772.
7. Ibid.

Thursday, December 18, 1862
1. *Official Records,* ser. 1, vol. 16, pt. 1, 798; Steger, 226.
2. Steger, 226; Steenburn, 144.
3. Steenburn, 144-45; Steger, 226; Cook, 54; *Official Records,* ser. 1, vol.17, pt. 1, 554-55.
4. Cook, 54.
5. Bradley, *Escort and Staff,* 54.
6. James Jones.
7. Morton, 53-54.
8. Rose, 132.
9. Barron, 133.
10. Hale, 144; Hartje, 258.
11. Jordan and Pryor, 197; *Official Records,* ser. 1, vol. 17, pt. 1, 512, 598.
12. Ayers, 22-23.

Friday, December 19, 1862

1. *Official Records,* ser. 1, vol. 17, pt. 1, 555-56, 592.
2. Ibid., vol. 23, pt. 2, 275-77, 498; Cadwallader, 34-35.
3. Hartje, 259-60; Carter, 133-34.
4. Cadwallader, 35.

Saturday, December 20, 1862

1. Carter, 137; Cadwallader, 36-37.
2. Carter, 134.
3. A. F. Brown, 6:157.
4. Hale, 145.
5. McMinn, 385-86.
6. Barron, 136-37.
7. Carter, 141-42.
8. Rose, 87.
9. Lowe, 221.
10. *Official Records,* ser. 1, vol. 17, pt. 1, 518, 508-9; Ibid., pt. 2, 439; Cadwallader, 36-37; Woodworth, 265.
11. Wyeth, *That Devil Forrest,* 101.
12. Hill-Freeman Camp.
13. Wyeth, *That Devil,* 101.
14. Hill-Freeman Camp.
15. Porter, 113-15; Warner, 76-77; Allardice, 73.
16. Duke, 200.

Sunday, December 21, 1862

1. *Official Records,* ser. 1, vol. 17, pt. 1, 521.
2. Lowe, 221-22.
3. Barron, 138-39.
4. Carter, 148.
5. Rose, 91.
6. Hale, 148.
7. *Official Records,* ser. 1, vol. 20, pt. 1, 131-32.
8. Ibid., vol. 17, pt. 1, 598.
9. Jordan and Pryor, 203; Bradley, "Crossing at Clifton," 13.
10. Wyeth, *That Devil Forrest,* 102.
11. Porter, 115.
12. Duke, 199.
13. Woodworth, 265; Simpson, 167. Simpson argues that foraging was easy and that Grant could have sustained the campaign by living off the land; Woodworth's argument is supported by the evidence that forage for men and animals was scarce along the route of the retreat.

14. Ayers, 23-24.

Monday, December 22, 1862
1. Henry, 114.
2. Wyeth, "Morgan's Christmas Raid," 144.
3. Porter, 116.
4. Barron, 140-41; Carter, 140.
5. Carter, 150.
6. Ayers, 24.

Tuesday, December 23, 1862
1. *Official Records,* ser. 1, vol. 17, pt. 1, 567-68.
2. Ibid., 159.
3. Porter, 116.
4. Carter, 151.

Wednesday, December 24, 1862
1. Wyeth, "Morgan's Christmas Raid," 146; Duke, 201.
2. *Official Records,* ser. 1, vol. 17, pt. 1, 523-24; Hale, 149.
3. *Official Records,* ser. 1, vol. 17, pt. 1, 484-85.
4. Carter, 154-55.

Thursday, December 25, 1862
1. Lytle, 127.
2. *Official Records,* ser. 1, vol. 17, pt. 1, 479.
3. Wyeth, "Morgan's Christmas Raid," 146-48.
4. Porter, 116-17.
5. *Official Records,* ser. 1, vol. 20, pt. 1, 137; Asher, 5.
6. Van Horne, 174-75.
7. Carter, 154-55.
8. *Official Records,* ser. 1, vol. 20, pt. 1, 519; Carter, 155; Lowe, 223; Barron, 141-42.
9. Dodson, 48. This book, originally published in 1899, was the first history of Wheeler's cavalry. Wheeler read the manuscript prior to its publication.
10. Ayers, 24.

Friday, December 26, 1862
1. Woodworth, 266.
2. *Official Records,* ser. 1, vol. 17, pt. 1, 137.
3. Ibid., 490-91; Maness, *Lightning Warfare,* 126-28; Morton, 61.
4. Van Horne, 174; Bearss, "Cavalry Operations," 1:27.
5. Carter, 156; *Official Records,* ser. 1, vol. 17, pt. 1, 520.

6. *Official Records,* ser. 1, vol. 20, pt. 1, 962.

7. Wyeth, "Morgan's Christmas Raid," 148.

8. Porter, 118-19.

9. Ibid.

10. Bearss, "West Tennessee," 40.

11. *Official Records,* ser. 1, vol. 20, pt. 1, 262, 269, 279, 347.

12. Dodson, 50.

Saturday, December 27, 1862

1. Bearss, "West Tennessee," 21.

2. Carter, 156-57.

3. Woodworth, 267; Ballard, 135.

4. *Official Records,* ser. 1, vol. 20, pt. 1, 962-63;Bush, 4.

6. Porter, 120.

7. Asher, 7; Duke, 203-4.

8. Dee Alexander Brown, 151.

9. Wyeth, *Sabre and Scalpel,* 185.

10. *Official Records,* ser. 1, vol. 20, pt. 1, 138; Ramage, 142.

11. *Official Records,* ser. 1, vol. 20, pt. 1, 253-54, 328-29.

Sunday, December 28, 1862

1. Maness, *Lightning Warfare,* 129; Wyeth, *That Devil Forrest,* 103-04.

2. *Official Records,* ser. 1, vol. 20, pt. 1, 963.

3. Ballard, 135.

4. Bush, 4; Asher, 5; *Official Records,* ser. 1, vol. 20, pt. 1, 156.

5. Wyeth, *Sabre and Scalpel,* 185-86.

6. Dee Alexander Brown, 152.

7. Porter, 121.

8. *Official Records,* ser. 1, vol. 20, pt. 1, 138.

9. Ibid., pt. 2, 467; Allardice, 346.

10. Ayers, 28.

Monday, December 29, 1862

1. Ballard, 141.

2. *Official Records,* ser. 1, vol. 20, pt. 1, 254, 263, 295, 347, 963.

3. Ibid., 958, 969.

4. Bearss, "Cavalry Operations," 1: 24-25.

5. *Official Records,* ser. 1, vol. 20, pt. 1, 663; Bearss, "Cavalry Operations," 1:53.

6. Maness, *Lightning Warfare,* 129.

7. Bearss, "West Tennessee," 21; Lytle, 131; Maness, *Lightning Warfare,* 132.

8. *Official Records,* ser. 1, vol. 20, pt. 1, 156.

9. Allardice, 96, 103.

10. *Official Records,* ser. 1, vol. 20, pt. 1, 139.

11. Ibid.; Asher, 7.

12. Porter, 121-23.

13. Dee Alexander Brown, 153-54; *Official Records,* ser. 1, vol. 20, pt. 1, 139.

14. Wyeth, *Sabre and Scalpel,* 187-88.

Tuesday, December 30, 1862

1. Maness, *Lightning Warfare,* 133, 199.

2. Beard, "West Tennessee," 307-8.

3. Maness, *Untutored Genius,* 101.

4. Bearss, "West Tennessee," 43; Maness, *Untutored Genius,* 101.

5. Ayers, 29.

6. *Official Records,* ser. 1, vol. 20, pt. 958-60.

7. Porter, 126; Wyeth, "Christmas Raid," 152; Wyeth, *Sabre and Scalpel,* 188-89.

8. *Official Records,* ser. 1, vol. 20, pt. 1, 959-60.

9. Ibid.

10. Dyer, 66-68.

11. McDonough, 78.

Wednesday, December 31, 1862

1. Bearss, "West Tennessee," 44.

2. Jordan and Pryor, 215-16.

3. Lytle, 132-33.

4. Beard, "Bravest of Brave," 367-68.

5. Kennerly, 41.

6. *Official Records,* ser. 1, vol. 17, pt. 1 586.

7. Lindsley, 796.

8. Peter.

9. *Official Records,* ser. 1, vol. 17, pt. 1, 586-89.

10. Wyeth, *That Devil Forrest,* 128.

11. Kennerly, 27-28; Bearss, "West Tennessee," 47.

12. Bearss, "West Tennessee," 47.

13. Henry, 118.

14. Allardice, 91. Another account has John Jackson, a member of Forrest's Escort, bringing the news that a Union force had arrived in Forrest's rear. In this account, Forrest goes to check on the report and is almost captured. He then returns to gather forces, which then make the charge. This account seems less likely than

the one having Carroll give the warning. The second account would have had Forrest riding more than a mile to view the attackers, returning to gather the forces, then riding almost another mile to get into position for the flank attack. Such an amount of riding would have given the U.S. forces time to do much more damage.

15. Wyeth, *That Devil Forrest,* 134-35.
16. Cited in Bradley, *Escort and Staff,* 60.
17. *Official Records,* ser. 1, vol. 17, pt. 1, 522.
18. "Parker's Crossroads."
19. Ayers, 30-32.
20. *Official Records,* ser. 1, vol. 20, pt. 1, 144.
21. Ibid., 157.
22. Ibid.; Wyeth, "Christmas Raid," 154-56.
23. Porter, 126.
24. Dyer, 66.
25. *Official Records,* ser. 1, vol. 20, pt. 1, 966.
26. Ibid.; Cozzens, 104.
27. *Official Records,* ser. 1, vol. 20, pt. 1, 966.
28. Murrah, 62.
29. Cozzens, 88; Murrah, 63-64.
30. *Official Records,* ser. 1, vol. 20, pt. 1, 967-68; Bearss, "Cavalry Operations," 1:122-23; Cozzens, 105-06.
31. Cozzens, 108.
32. Poole, 64-65.

Thursday, January 1, 1863
1. *Official Records,* ser. 1, vol. 17, pt. 1 590-91, 599; Wyeth, *That Devil Forrest,* 120.
2. Sensing, 133-36.
3. *Official Records,* ser. 1, vol. 20, pt. 1, 146.
4. Bearss, "Cavalry Operations," 2:131-32.
5. *Official Records,* ser. 1, vol. 20, pt. 1, 655-56.
6. Ibid., vol. 17, pt. 1, 599.
7. Ayers, 33.

Friday, January 2, 1863
1. Kennerly, 43; Bearss, "West Tennessee," 48.
2. *Official Records,* ser. 1, vol. 20, pt. 1, 158; Ramage, 144.
3. Bearss, "Cavalry Operations," 2:137.

Saturday, January 3, 1863
1. Bearss, "West Tennessee," 48.

2. *Official Records,* ser. 1, vol. 20, pt. 1, 158.

Aftermath and Results
1. Bradley, *Escort and Staff,* 62. See also Bradley, *With Blood and Fire.*

Appendix A: The Horsemen of the Confederate Raids
1. Allardice, 350.
2. Horn, 2:62.
3. Lindsley, 627ff.
4. Warner, 72-73.
5. Horn, 1:83.
6. Lindsley, 651ff.
7. Horn, 1:38.
8. Ibid., 76.
9. Ibid., 44-45.
10. Bradley, *Escort and Staff,* 14.
11. Allardice, 330.
12. Bradley, *They Rode with Forrest*, 25.
13. Horn, 1:131-32.
14. Ibid., 140-42.
15. Warner, 76-77.
16. Kentucky Legislature.
17. Duke, 344ff.
18. Allardice, 103.
19. "Palmer's Battery."
20. Allardice, 73.
21. Duke, 197-98.
22. "Ninth Kentucky."
23. Warner, 156.
24. Johnson, 309ff.
25. Allardice, 96.
26. Quisenberry, 259-89.
27. Horn, 1:74-76.
28. Allardice, 174-75.
29. Rose, 78ff. See also Barron and Hale.
30. Horn, 1:69-71.
31. Allardice, 39.
32. Horn, 1:66-68.
33. Allardice, 240.
34. Rowland, 762ff.
35. Allardice, 261-62.

36. Horn, 1:49ff.
37. Ibid., 40-41.
38. Ibid., 43.
39. Ibid., 80.
40. Bradley, *They Rode with Forrest,* 43.
41. Ibid., 80.
42. Poole, 193.

Bibliography

Allardice, Bruce S. *Confederate Colonels: A Biographical Register.* Columbia, MO: University of Missouri Press, 2008.

Asher, Tim. "John Hunt Morgan's Christmas Raid." Paper for the Hardin County History Museum. http://www.hardinkyhistory.org/morgan.pdf.

Ayers, O. C. "This Looks But Little Like Trying to Catch the Enemy: A Union Lieutenant Pursues General Forrest." Edited by Dale Snair. *Civil War Times Illustrated* 23, no. 5 (September 1984): 20-33.

Ballard, Michael B. *Vicksburg: The Campaign That Opened the Mississippi.* Chapel Hill: University of North Carolina Press, 2004.

Barron, S. B. *The Lone Star Defenders: A Chronicle of the 3rd Texas Cavalry, Ross' Brigade.* New York: Neale, 1908.

Beard, Dan W. "Forrest's Men Rank with Bravest of Brave." *Southern Historical Society Papers* (Richmond, VA) 37 (1909): 364-68. Reprint, Wilmington, NC: Broadfoot, 1991.

———. "With Forrest in West Tennessee: Winter Campaign of 1862 Filled With Adventures and Incidents." *Southern Historical Society Papers* (Richmond, VA) 37 (1909): 304-8. Reprint, Wilmington, NC: Broadfoot, 1991.

Bearss, Edwin C. "Cavalry Operations in the Battle of Stones River." Parts 1 and 2. *Tennessee Historical Quarterly* 19, no. 1 (1960): 23-53; no. 2 (1960): 110-44.

———. "Forrest's West Tennessee Campaign of 1862 and the Battle of Parker's Cross-Road." *Blue and Gray Magazine* 20, no. 6 (2003).

Bradley, Michael R. *Crossing at Clifton.* Privately printed, 2004.

———. *Nathan Bedford Forrest's Escort and Staff.* Gretna, LA: Pelican, 2006.

———. *They Rode with Forrest.* Gretna, LA: Pelican, 2012.

———. *With Blood and Fire: Life Behind Union Lines in Middle Tennessee, 1863-65.* Shippensburg, PA: Burd Street, 2000.

Brown, A. F. "Van Dorn's Operations in Northern Mississippi—Recollections of a Cavalryman." *Southern Historical Society Papers* 6 (1878): 151-61.

Brown, Dee Alexander. *The Bold Cavaliers: Morgan's 2nd Kentucky Cavalry Raiders.* Philadelphia: J. B. Lippincott, 1959.

Bush, Bryan S. "Morgan's Christmas Raid." Bryan S. Bush Books, 2009. http://www.bryansbush.com/hub.php?page=articles&layer=a0912.

Cadwallader, Sylvanus. *Three Years With Grant.* New York: Alfred A. Knopf, 1955.

Carter, Arthur B. *The Tarnished Cavalier: Major General Earl Van Dorn, C.S.A.* Knoxville: University of Tennessee Press, 1999.

Cook, V. Y. "Forrest's Capture of Col. R. G. Ingersoll," *Confederate Veteran* 15 (February 1907): 54-55.

Cozzens, Peter. *No Better Place to Die: The Battle of Stones River.* Urbana: University of Illinois Press, 1991.

Daniel, Larry J. *Days of Glory: The Army of the Cumberland, 1861-1865.* Baton Rouge: Louisiana State University Press, 2006.

Dodson, W. C. *Campaigns of Wheeler and His Cavalry, 1862-1865: From Material Furnished by Gen. Joseph Wheeler to which is Added His Concise and Graphic Account of the Santiago Campaign of 1898.* Atlanta: Hudgins, 1899. Reprint, Memphis: E. F. Williams and J. J. Fox, 1997.

Duke, Basil Wilson. *History of Morgan's Cavalry.* 1867. Reprint, Dayton: General Books, 2009.

Dyer, John P. *From Shiloh to San Juan: The Life of "Fightin' Joe" Wheeler.* Baton Rouge: Louisiana State University Press, 1941.

Hale, Douglas. *The Third Texas Cavalry in the Civil War.* Norman: University of Oklahoma Press, 1993.

Hartje, Robert G. *Van Dorn: The Life and Times of a Confederate General.* Nashville: Vanderbilt University Press, 1967.

Henry, Robert Selph. *"First With the Most" Forrest.* Jackson, TN: McCowan-Mercer, 1969.

Hill-Freeman Camp, Sons of Confederate Veterans. *Driving Tour of the Battle of Trenton.* Author's Collection, 1985.

Horn, Stanley F. *Tennesseans in the Civil War.* 2 Vols. Nashville: Civil War Centennial Commission, 1964.

Hyneman, D. J. "Scouting Around Holly Springs." *Confederate Veteran* 21 (1913): 586.

Johnson, Adam Rankin. *The Partisan Rangers of the Confederate States Army.* Austin: State House, 1995.

Jones, James. "Lacy Correspondence: January 7, 1863." *The Civil War Sourcebook: An Online Civil War Resource.* http://tennessee.civilwarsourcebook.com.

Jones, Shirley Farris. "Martha Ready Morgan: From Wife to Widow in 630 Days." *Murfreesboro (TN) Post.* January 6, 2008. http://www.murfreesboropost.com/martha-ready-morgan-from-wife-to-widow-in-630-days-cms-8283.

Jordan, Thomas, and J. P. Pryor. *The Campaigns of General Nathan Bedford Forrest and of Forrest's Cavalry.* 1868. Reprint, New York: Da Capo, 1996.

Kennerly, Dan. *Forrest at Parker's Crossroads: The Dawn of Lightening War.* 7th ed. Richmond, TX: Parker's Crossroads, 2001.

Kentucky Legislature. *Report of the Adjutant General of the State of Kentucky: 1861-1866.* 1866. Reprint, Utica, KY: McDowell, 1984.

Lindsley, John Berrien. *The Military Annals of Tennessee: Confederate. First Series, Embracing a Review of Military Operations, with Regimental Histories and Memorial Rolls.* 1886. Reprint, Wilmington, NC: Broadfoot, 1995.

Lowe, Richard, ed. *A Texas Cavalry Officer's Civil War: The Diary and Letters of James C. Bates.* Baton Rouge: LSU Press, 1999.

Lytle, Andrew Nelson. *Bedford Forrest and His Critter Company.* 1931. Reprint, Nashville: J. S. Sanders, 1992.

McDonough, James Lee. *Stones River: Bloody Winter in Tennessee.* Knoxville: University of Tennessee Press, 1980.

McMinn, W. P. "Service with Van Dorn's Cavalry." *Confederate Veteran* 27 (1919): 384-86.

McWhiney, Grady, and Judith Lee Hallock. *Braxton Bragg and Confederate Defeat.* 2 vols. Tuscaloosa: University of Alabama Press, 1969.

Maness, Lonnie E. *An Untutored Genius: The Military Career of General Nathan Bedford Forrest.* Oxford, MS: Guild Bindery, 1990.

———. *Lightning Warfare: Forrest's First West Tennessee Campaign, December, 1862.* Jackson, TN: Main Street, 2007.

Morton, John Watson. *The Artillery of Nathan Bedford Forrest's Cavalry.* 1909. Reprint, Marietta, GA: R. Bemis, 1995

Murrah, Jeffrey D. *None but Texans: A History of Terry's Texas Rangers.* Austin: Eakin, 2001.

"Ninth Kentucky." *Ninth Kentucky Cavalry.* http://ninethkentucky.org.

Official Records of the War of the Rebellion. 119 vols.
Washington, DC: United States War Department, 1899.

"Palmer's Battery." *The War Between the States.* http://
warbetweenthestates.com.

"Parker's Crossroads," *Confederate Veteran* 16 (March 1908):
338.

Parks, Joseph H. *General Leonidas Polk, C. S. A.: The Fighting
Bishop.* Baton Rouge: Louisiana State University Press, 1962.

Peter, William H. Letter to his parents, 4 January 1863. Illinois
Historical Society, Springfield, IL.

Poole, John Randolph. *Cracker Cavaliers: The 2nd Georgia
Cavalry Under Wheeler and Forrest.* Macon, GA: Mercer
University Press, 2000.

Porter, John M. *One of Morgan's Men: Memoirs of Lieutenant
John M. Porter of the Ninth Kentucky Cavalry.* Edited by Kent
Masterson Brown. Lexington: University Press of Kentucky,
2011.

Quisenberry, Anderson Chenault. "The Eleventh Kentucky
Cavalry, CSA." *Southern Historical Society Papers* (Richmond,
VA) 35 (1907): 259-89. Reprint, Wilmington, NC: Broadfoot,
1991.

Ramage, James A. *Rebel Raider: The Life of General John Hunt
Morgan.* Lexington: University Press of Kentucky, 1986.

Rose, Victor M. *Ross' Texas Brigade.* 1881. Reprint, La Vergne,
TN: Kessinger, 2011.

Rowland, Dunbar. *The Official and Statistical Register of the
State of Mississippi.* 1908. Reprint, Salem, MA: Higginson,
1995.

Sensing, Thurman. *Champ Ferguson, Confederate Guerrilla.*
Nashville: Vanderbilt University Press, 1942.

Simpson, Brooks D. *Ulysses S. Grant: Triumph over Adversity,
1822-1865.* Boston: Houghton-Mifflin, 2000.

Steenburn, Donald H. *The Man Called Gurley.* Meridianville, AL:
Elk River, 1999.

Steger, J. C. "The Cavalry Fight at Lexington, Tenn." *Confederate
Veteran* 15 (1907): 226.

Van Horne, Thomas B. *History of the Army of the Cumberland:
Its Organization, Campaigns, Battles, Written at the Request
of General George H. Thomas.* 1875. Reprint, New York:
Smithmark, 1996.

Warner, Ezra J. *Generals in Gray: Lives of the Confederate
Commanders.* Baton Rouge: LSU Press, 1959.

West, Mike. "The President's Coming . . . to Old Murfreesboro." *Murfreesboro (TN) Post.* November 29, 2009. http://www. murfreesboropost.com/the-presidents-coming-to-old-murfreesborough-cms-20637.

West, Mike, "'The Wedding' Still Captivates after 144 Years." *Murfreesboro (TN) Post.* December 10, 2006. http://www. murfreesboropost.com/the-wedding-still-captivates-after-144-years-cms-1208.

Woodworth, Steven. *Nothing but Victory: The Army of the Tennessee, 1861-1865.* New York: Alfred A. Knopf, 2005.

Wyeth, John Allan. "Morgan's Christmas Raid, 1862-63." Edited by Francis T. Miller. *The Photographic History of the Civil War.* New York: Review of Reviews, 1911.

———. *That Devil Forrest: Life of General Nathan Bedford Forrest.* 1899. Reprint, Baton Rouge: LSU Press, 1959.

———. *With Sabre and Scalpel: The Autobiography of a Soldier and Surgeon.* New York: Harper & Brothers, 1914.

Index

A
Alexandria, Tennessee, 66, 72, 75
Allen, William W., 173
Anderson, Charles, 50, 87
Anderson, Paul F., 179
Ashby, H. M., 178
Ayers, Oliver C., 53, 73, 77, 91, 133, 148

B
Barron, S. B., 61
Bates, James, 63
Bath Springs, Tennessee, 41
Baxter, Nat, 126, 129, 131
Bennett, James D., 67
Biffle, J. B., 21, 55, 65, 94, 120
Boggess, Jiles S., 24, 170
Bolivar, Tennessee, 52, 77, 81, 84-85
Bragg, Braxton, 19-20, 22, 27-28, 33-34, 38, 41, 73, 98, 111, 113-14,
    120, 140, 152, 156
Breckinridge, William Campbell Preston, 67, 166
Broocks, John H., 24, 170
Buckner, Simon Bolivar, 28
Buford, Abraham, 114
Butler, J. R., 179
Burkesville, Kentucky, 149

C
Carroll, Charles, 130
Carter, James Epps, 174
Chattanooga, Tennessee, 31
Cheatham, Benjamin Franklin, 33
Chenault, David Waller, 67, 116, 168

Clanton, James, 173
Clark County Artillery. *See* Wiggins's Arkansas Battery
Clarksburg, Tennessee, 125
Cleburne, Patrick, 25, 104
Clifton, Tennessee, 21-22, 28-29, 31, 37, 46, 115, 145, 148-49, 151
Cluke, Leroy Stuart, 67, 116, 165
Cluke's Scouts, 122
Columbus, Kentucky, 73, 79, 83, 88, 145
Corbett, C. C., 67
Corbett's Battery, 169
Corinth, Mississippi, 19
Cowan, J. B., 50
Cox, John T., 177
Cox, Nicholas Nichols, 28-29, 53, 101, 115, 130, 132, 152, 160
Cox's Cavalry Battalion, 65, 160-61
Crittenden, T. T., 47
Cummings, H. J. B., 128

D
Darcyville, Tennessee, 80
Davis, John R., 157, 179
Davis, Jefferson, 19-20, 27, 31, 38, 70-71, 88, 98
Davis, Thomas, 88
Davis's Mills, Mississippi, 69
Davis's Tennessee Battalion. *See* Tennessee Battalion (Davis)
Dibrell, George Gibbs, 21, 53, 64, 71-72, 128, 130, 132, 145, 148, 158
Dickey, T. Lyle, 34, 57
Douglass, DeWitt Clinton, 174
Douglass's Tennessee Battalion. *See* Tennessee Battalion (Douglass)
Dresden, Tennessee, 94
Duke, Basil Wilson, 34, 67, 73, 89, 103, 109, 116-18, 164
Dunham, Cyrus, 111, 120, 125-32

E
Eighth Confederate Cavalry, 114, 123, 174
Eighth Kentucky Cavalry, 67, 165
Eighth Tennessee Cavalry, 21, 71, 158-60, 178
Eighth Texas Cavalry, 80, 114, 141-42
Eleventh Kentucky Cavalry, 67, 116, 168
Eleventh Tennessee Cavalry, 174-75
Elizabethtown, Kentucky, 103

Ellsworth, George, 96
Englemann, Adolph, 55
Estes, William N., 177

F
Ferguson, Champ, 146
Fifth Kentucky Cavalry, 179
Fifty-First Alabama Cavalry, 90, 96, 102, 114, 173
First Alabama Cavalry, 38, 114, 173
First Confederate Cavalry, 114, 177
First Georgia Cavalry, 114, 176
First Georgia Infantry, 166
First Kentucky Cavalry, 179
First Louisiana Cavalry, 114, 176
First Mississippi Cavalry, 60-61, 171
First Tennessee Cavalry, 114, 171, 174
First Tennessee Infantry, 175
First Texas Cavalry, 170
First Texas Legion, 170
Flake's Store, Tennessee, 115, 119, 125
Forrest, Jeffrey, 53
Forrest, Nathan Bedford, 20-24, 28-32, 37, 41, 45-47, 49-50, 52-53, 55-56, 64-66, 70-73, 75, 77, 79-80, 83-84, 87-88, 94, 98, 101, 107, 115, 119-20, 125-27, 129-33, 143, 145, 148-49, 151-53, 155-57, 161
Forrest, William, 120
Fourteenth Alabama Battalion, 114, 177
Fourteenth Tennessee Cavalry, 67, 168
Fourth Alabama Cavalry, 21, 49, 53, 64, 162
Fourth Tennessee Cavalry, 21, 114, 157-58, 178-79
Franklin, Tennessee, 111
Freeman, Samuel L., 21, 28, 31, 37, 51, 65-66, 70, 72, 132, 149, 163
Freeman's Battery, 55, 163
Fry, Jacob, 65
Fuller, John W., 129-32, 151

G
Gaines, F. Y., 173
Gallatin, Tennessee, 89, 93
Glasgow, Kentucky, 84
Grand Junction, Tennessee, 76-77, 85

Grant, Ulysses S., 19, 22-23, 25, 30, 34, 42, 46-47, 52, 55, 57, 59-60, 63-64, 69, 73, 76-77, 83, 85-86, 93-94, 96-98, 101-2, 108, 113, 154

Graves, William, 84

Grayport, Mississippi, 101

Green River, Kentucky, 88, 146

Grenada, Mississippi, 23, 29, 32, 37, 42

Grenfell, St. Leger, 73

Grierson, Benjamin, 64, 77, 85-86, 89-90, 154

Griffith, John Summerfield, 23-24, 169

Grigsby, J. W., 180

Gurley, Frank, 45-46, 49

H

Halisy, Dennis J., 139-40

Halleck, Henry, 83, 88

Hanson, Roger, 33

Hardee, William, 33, 141

Harlan, John, 89, 93-94, 104, 110-11, 116-18

Harrisburg, Mississippi, 48

Haskins, W. A., 139

Hawkins, E. R., 24, 170

Holly Springs, Mississippi, 22-24, 32, 42, 46-47, 52, 57, 59-60, 62-63, 69-70, 73, 76-77, 85, 88, 90, 101, 108

Holman's Tennessee Battalion. *See* Tennessee Battalion (Holman)

Houston, Mississippi, 46

Huddleton, Elam, 146

Huff, J. M., 165

Huggins, Amariah L., 163

Humboldt, Tennessee, 53, 73, 77, 91, 98

Hutchinson, John B., 67, 165

Huwald's Tennessee Battery, 114

Hyneman, D. J., 42

I

Ingersoll, Robert G., 46, 50

J

Jackson, John, 161

Jackson, Tennessee, 52-53, 55, 73, 83

Jackson, William Hicks, 23, 170

Jefferson, Tennessee, 121

John Jackson's Cavalry Company, 161
Johnson, Adam R., 67, 166
Johnson's Plantation, Mississippi, 93
Johnston, Joseph E., 20, 27

K
Kennett, John, 95
Kenton Station, Tennessee, 75, 79
Kirk, Benjamin, 141

L
Lacy, A. J., 51
La Vergne, Tennessee, 47, 96, 122, 146
Lawton, Winburn Joseph, 177
Lebanon, Kentucky, 139
Lee, Stephen Dill, 102
Lexington, Tennessee, 49, 148, 153
Lindsay, Andrew Jackson, 171
Little, Montgomery, 161
Locks Mill, Tennessee, 76
Logan, Samuel, 79, 85
Louisville & Nashville Railroad, 94, 96, 103, 109, 154
Lumpkin's Plantation, 59

M
McCollum, Alexander S., 143
McCook, Alexander McDowell, 105, 141, 152
McCulloch, Robert M., 23, 171-72
McGuire, John W. H., 49
McKenzie, Tennessee, 101
McLemore, William Sugars, 125-26, 129-30, 158
Malone, James C., 177
Mason, Courtland, 109
Memphis & Charleston Railroad, 19, 57, 76
Middleburg, Tennessee, 84-85
Milroy, Robert, 155
Minty, Robert H. G., 95
Mississippi Central Railroad, 52-53, 55, 60, 69, 76, 85
Mizner, John K., 64, 86, 97
Mobile & Ohio Railroad, 19, 21, 34, 42, 46, 48, 51-53, 55, 65, 75, 79, 87
Morgan, George Washington, 113

Morgan, John Hunt, 20, 27, 30, 33-34, 39, 42, 66-67, 69-70, 72, 75, 80, 84, 88-89, 93-94, 96, 103-4, 109-11, 114-18, 122, 139, 145-46, 149, 151-53, 156, 164
Morgan, John T., 173
Morgan, William H., 69
Morrison, James J., 176
Morton, John Watson, 28, 37, 51, 64, 94, 109, 149, 163
Morton's Battery, 126, 163
Muldraugh Hill, Kentucky, 109
Munfordville, Kentucky, 104, 110
Murfreesboro, Tennessee, 19, 27, 31, 33-34, 38, 41, 47, 73, 89, 95-96, 98-99, 102, 105, 108, 111, 113-14, 121-22, 124, 140, 142-43, 147, 150-52, 154
Murphy, Robert, 59
Murray, John P., 179
Murray's Tennessee Regiment. *See* Tennessee Regiment (Murray)

N
Napier, Thomas Alonzo, 94, 161
Napier's Cavalry Battalion, 161
Nashville, Tennessee, 47, 56, 71, 89, 95
New Albany, Mississippi, 52, 97
Nimmo, J., 59
Nineteenth Battalion. *See* Seventh Alabama Cavalry
Ninth Kentucky Cavalry, 67, 84, 88, 97, 166
Ninth Tennessee Cavalry, 21
Ninth Texas Cavalry, 63, 69, 90
Nolensville, Tennessee, 80, 90, 98

O
Oxford, Mississippi, 57, 60, 63, 77, 98

P
Paine, Eleazar, 155
Palmer, Joseph, 166
Palmer's Georgia Battery, 67, 165
Parker's Crossroads, 32, 120, 125-27, 129-33, 148, 153
Pegram, John, 42, 114
Pemberton, John C., 20, 22-24, 38
Pinson, R. A., 172
Polk, Leonidas, 28, 34
Pontotoc, Mississippi, 39, 46, 51, 55, 57

Porter, John, 72, 88, 97

Q
Quirk's Scouts, 84, 88, 96, 118

R
Ready, Charles, Jr., 33
Ready, Martha, 33
Red Mound, Tennessee, 130
Ripley, Mississippi, 57, 59, 90
Rolling Fork River, 115, 139
Rosecrans, William Starke, 22, 27, 38, 41, 56, 71, 89, 94-96, 98,
    114-15, 118, 121-23, 140, 142-44, 146-47, 152, 154
Russell, A. A., 21, 45, 49, 53, 64, 101, 107, 115, 128, 131-32, 162

S
Saulsbury, Tennessee, 89
Scott, John Sims, 176
Second Arkansas Light Artillery. *See* Wiggins's Arkansas Battery
Second Georgia Cavalry, 80, 114, 177
Second Kentucky Cavalry, 164
Second Missouri Cavalry, 172
Second Tennessee Cavalry, 114, 178
Seventh Alabama Cavalry, 177
Seventh Tennessee Cavalry, 170
Shady Hill, Tennessee, 45
Sherman, William T., 23, 93-94, 102, 109, 113
Shiloh, Battle of, 19
Sixteenth Tennessee Battalion, 114
Sixth Kentucky Cavalry, 180
Sixth Texas Cavalry, 62, 170
Smith, Baxter, 25, 111, 178-79
Smithville, Tennessee, 151
Somerville, Tennessee, 76
Spring Creek, Tennessee, 64
Springfield, Kentucky, 122, 139
Spring Hill, Tennessee, 155, 159, 162-64, 171
Stanley, David, 95
Starkweather, John C., 122
Starnes, James Wellborn, 21, 28, 65, 119-20, 128, 131, 132, 157
Stevens, S. H., 32
Stocks, John G., 170

Stoner, Robert G., 67
Strange, John, 66, 129
Sullivan, Jeremiah, 22, 73, 83, 94, 98, 107, 115, 129-30, 132, 138, 149

T
Tennessee Battalion (Davis), 114, 179
Tennessee Battalion (Douglass), 114, 174-75
Tennessee Battalion (Holman), 114, 174-75
Tennessee Cavalry, 23
Tennessee Regiment (Murray), 114, 178
Tenth Kentucky Cavalry, 67, 167
Tenth Tennessee Cavalry, 53
Texas Cavalry Brigade, 23-24, 60-61, 63, 85
Third Alabama Cavalry, 114, 173
Third Confederate Cavalry, 114, 177
Third Georgia Cavalry, 114, 178
Third Kentucky Cavalry, 165, 179
Third Texas Cavalry, 61, 170
Thurston, Gates P., 142
Tompkinsville, Kentucky, 80
Trenton, Tennessee, 65, 70-73, 75, 94, 98, 111, 115, 120, 132, 153
Triune, Tennessee, 104
Twelfth Tennessee Battalion, 114

U
Union City, Tennessee, 79, 84, 87
Upton, Kentucky, 96

V
Van Dorn, Earl, 22-24, 29-30, 37-38, 42, 46, 52, 57, 59-60, 62-64, 69-71, 76-77, 80, 84-86, 89-90, 97-98, 101-2, 108, 113, 152-53, 155

W
Wade, William Bartee, 174
Walker, Moses, 123
Walnut Hills, Mississippi, 102, 108, 113
Water Valley, Mississippi, 34
Webb, J. D., 96, 102
Webb's Station, 53
Wharton, John A., 24-25, 42, 62, 80, 95, 98, 104, 114, 140-43, 147

Wharton, John Mason "Jack," 24, 62, 170
Wharton's Escort Company, 179
Wheeler, Joseph, 25, 31, 41-42, 47, 71, 80, 95-96, 99, 114, 121-23, 140, 143, 147, 150-53, 155-56
Wheeler, James Thaddeus, 171
White's Section, 169
White's Tennessee Battery, 114
Wiggins, Jannedens H., 175
Wiggins's Arkansas Battery, 114, 175

Y
Yocknapatalfa River, 55

Z
Zahm, Lewis, 95, 142, 146-47, 152